Great American Catholics

Great American Catholics

by **Mary Ann Clark**
Jerri Pogue
Diane Rickard

Illustrations by
Robert L. Mutchler

Ave Maria Press • Notre Dame, Indiana 46556

Nihil Obstat: Rev. Edward Hanahoe, S.A.
            Censor Deputatus
Imprimatur: Most Rev. Thomas J. Welsh, D.D.
            Bishop of Arlington

Library of Congress Catalog Card Number: 76-7278
International Standard Book Number: 0-87793-111-9

Contents

To all of the Christ-like people
who made a difference in our lives . . .
especially . . . Robert Audley and David Byrnes

Introduction

Countless numbers of people have made and continue to make noteworthy contributions to our American heritage. Throughout this era of celebration (from 1976, the anniversary of the signing of the Declaration of Independence, to 1989, the anniversary of the signing of the Constitution), a great deal of attention will be given to our forebears through radio and TV spots.

This book has been developed to make available enrichment material concerning the particular role Catholics have played and continue to play in the development of our American tradition and heritage. Our primary goal is to indicate that the commitment and insight of Catholic Christians have been significant forces in the shaping of American thought. At the same time we want to point out how American ideals have and do influence our Catholic consciousness.

We are very much aware of the fact that the distance between the general knowledge we have of Catholic American history and the detailed expertise others hold is considerable! Nevertheless, we thought it important for youngsters and adults to have some historical sense of what it means to be a Catholic American. One way to encourage this sensitivity is to look at great Catholic Americans from the past and to examine the way they lived their lives. This we decided to do and, because the study of history is essentially the story of people, we chose the biographical approach.

Though there are many more lives deserving such investigation we picked 21 people who, we think, made significant contributions to our history and who suggest designs for new styles of living as Catholic Christians. We selected people we wanted our sons and daughters to know about. Among them are priests, sisters, lay people—married and single, those born into the Catholic tradition and converts. They generally fall into three main categories: those born in America, those born in Europe who became naturalized United States citizens, those whose major work was accomplished in this "new" land, though they remained Europeans.

Through short biographical sketches we highlight one theme running through each person's life, a theme which affected his or her decision-making. It would be ideal if teachers could become sufficiently familiar with the data to be able to tell the stories in their own words. For variety, teachers may want to tape the biographies and then play them for the youngsters. Often an interested student is happy to have the chance to make a "special report" by reading the data, digesting it and then retelling it to the class. Other suggestions for help in presenting the biographies would include the use of flannel boards, puppet shows, write-on slides, an overhead projector, duplicating materials or dramatic readings.

Each story is followed by learning experiences which contain directions for creative activities adapted to a particular grade level. These activities are designed to deepen the students' understanding of the person presented in the biography. We developed activities we know our own youngsters are capable of and enjoy doing. They can be utilized in various ways — full class periods, short spots, as part of learning center activities, or projects for individual study and enrichment. They can easily be adapted for use outside the classroom. Parents may want to use this material with their youngsters at home.

At the end of each unit there is a liturgical celebration for classroom use or a home prayer service. In preparation, simply choose songs from those suggested and have youngsters rehearse the readings. One individual could read the theme while another lights a candle. Invite everybody to sing the opening song or to listen to it on a recording. Then pray the penitential rite together; listen to the readings; allow a moment for reflection and meditation; close with a song everybody knows and enjoys.

All this brings us to the questions: How is this book used? Where does it fit in? Whom is it for?

- Parish religious education programs for young people
- Catholic grade and junior high schools
- Parents with their youngsters at home
- Homilists
- The social studies program in parochial schools
- Parish or diocesan bicentennial celebration coordinators

The three of us want to thank all those who have helped in any way to make this book possible, and we are especially grateful to the many people who have continually assured us that this work is necessary and important. We owe much to Rev. Carl J. Pfeifer, S.J., Sister Janaan Manternach, O.S.F., and Andrea Kerr for editing the material and for their constructive criticism which helped to clarify these ideas for more effective sharing.

UNIT I

Era of Exploration and Colonization

Isaac Jogues (1607-1646)
and the North American Martyrs

"How are they to hear if no one preaches . . ."
—Romans 10:14

For centuries before the first Europeans visited the area that was to become the United States, Indians in a rich variety of cultures inhabited the land. They hunted and fished and lived in villages where great cities now stand. For hundreds of years the Indian way of life was "the American way," yet these native American civilizations are touched on only briefly in a typical study of this country's history.

Generally we think of North American history beginning in the 1500's and 1600's when Europeans, and particularly the French, brought their civilization across the Atlantic. At the time when medieval, Church-oriented society was dissolving in Western Europe, the French took possession of the Saint Lawrence River (1534) and sent explorers, trappers, traders and missionaries westward to claim the whole Mississippi River Valley.

In 1608 Samuel de Champlain established the most significant of the early French settlements, Quebec. Here Frenchmen came to barter and to build, to preach and to die. The first missionaries were the Franciscan Recollets but, awed by the possible mission opportunities among the Indians, they soon sought help from a larger order, the Jesuits.

In 1625 the French Jesuit priest Jean de Brébeuf began his work among the Huron Indians. By mastering the language and following their diet, he managed to win their confidence. But when Quebec was conquered by the English attack of 1629, Brébeuf was forced to return to France, along with all other French missionaries and traders. The political reversal was brief, however, and in 1633, when Champlain was permitted to sail for Canada, Jean de Brébeuf accompanied him back to Quebec. There,

13

joined by other newly arrived missionaries, he resumed the work begun eight years before.

By 1634 Father Brébeuf had reinstated himself among the Hurons and was comforting the sick, instructing the young and, when possible, baptizing. He worked among the Indians until 1649 when, in the midst of the Iroquois destruction of the Huron nation, he was captured and tortured to death. His death is linked with the martyrdom of seven other Frenchmen—five Jesuits: Isaac Jogues, Charles Garnier, Anthony Daniel, Gabriel Lalemant, Noël Chabanel; and two laymen: René Goupil and John de LaLande. These last two were known as *donnes,* men who shared the work of the Jesuits but did not take their vows. All died between 1642 and 1649. Together these eight Frenchmen are known as the North American Martyrs.

They ministered to the Indians of northeastern North America and worked among the Huron, Petun, Neutral, Algonquin and Iroquois nations. By living singly and in pairs in the native villages, all had a share in the dream of converting the Indians. Each had sacrificed every comfort and security for the chance to spread the Good News of Jesus Christ among his Indian brothers and sisters.

Isaac Jogues, one of the North American martyrs, was born in Orléans, France, which Saint Joan of Arc had liberated from the English during the Hundred Years' War. There on January 10, 1607, Laurent Jogues, a prominent city official, and his wife, Francoise de Saint-Mesmin Jogues, celebrated the birth of their son, Isaac. They wondered what profession he would choose for himself. There were already lawyers, notaries, and apothecaries in the family — perhaps he would follow in the footsteps of one of these.

Young Isaac Jogues studied with private tutors until he was 10. Then he was sent to a Jesuit school. In 1624, when he graduated from college, he knew he wanted to become a priest. He entered the Jesuit novitiate at Rouen soon afterwards. The next year he went to the Royal College of La Fleche where he studied philosophy for three years. It was there that he met Father Enemond Masse, a missionary who had just spent two years in New France working among the people of Acadia and the Indians near Quebec. Father Masse is credited with being influential in causing Isaac Jogues to consider seriously the possibility of becoming a missionary.

When Jogues completed his philosophy degree, he taught for three years at the College of Rouen and then studied theology at Clermont College in Paris. In 1636 he was ordained and celebrated his first Mass on February 10, in Orléans. Two months later, on April 8, 1636, he sailed for the four-year-old Indian mission in Quebec.

A short time after his arrival, Father Jogues was sent to the Jesuit mission located in the Indian village, Ihonatira, to work among the Huron Indians. Other missionaries had been working in the same area for some time and knew well the problems involved in establishing missions and converting the Indians. Jogues' first task was to learn the Huron language; his teacher was Father Jean de Brébeuf. Jogues carefully studied Father Brébeuf's *Instruction*—a collection of data based on his years of living among the Indians. The notebook was helpful in preparing Jogues and other missionaries for many situations — both predictable and unexpected.

Father Jogues lived among the Hurons for six years. He taught them about Christ and the Church, and he found that they could memorize the catechism questions and answers quickly. He shared his food with his Indian brothers and sisters when they were hungry, and he cared for them when they were ill.

In 1642 Isaac Jogues and some companions, including René Goupil, went to Quebec to get new supplies. On the second day of their return trip they were attacked by a Mohawk war party, and, as prisoners, were taken on a tour of the Mohawk villages. The journey was a succession of savage tortures. Father Jogues was beaten and cut; his fingers were mangled. When the Mohawks finally tired of torturing Father Jogues, they made him a slave. For over a year he worked in the fields with the Mohawk women. Occasionally he and the other Frenchmen would go into the woods to pray and meditate. On September 29, 1642, as Jogues and René Goupil were returning to the village, Goupil was attacked and killed, becoming the first North American martyr. A year later, in December, 1643, Jogues escaped and the Dutch at Fort Orange helped him return to France. His superiors wanted him to stay in France to teach or write but they left the final decision up to him. His decision was firm — he wanted to convert the Mohawks, the Indians who had tortured him!

Early in 1644 Jogues sailed to Montreal, and ministered again to the Hurons while waiting for a chance to return to the Mohawks. Two years later he was sent to Ossernenon, the principal Mohawk village, to negotiate a peace agreement between the Iroquois Nation — of which the Mohawks were a part — and the French. After meeting for a week Jogues left for Quebec with news of success and a plan to return again to Ossernenon.

Unfortunately, the Mohawks had poor crops that year, and an epidemic broke out. They believed that the box containing vestments and religious articles which Jogues had left behind caused these disasters. As he was returning to the village from Quebec with John de LaLande and some Hurons, some members of the Mohawks' Bear clan captured the party. While a tribal council was being held to determine their fate the Bear clan invited Jogues to a dinner. As he stooped to enter their longhouse on October 19, 1646, he was tomahawked to death. The next day they also killed LaLande.

Father Isaac Jogues and the other missionaries of New France were men of great faith and courage. Unconcerned about personal risks, they went among the tribes telling their brothers and sisters about Christ. The sufferings they quietly endured remain one of the most heroic chapters in our past.

Recommended Readings

Kittler, Glenn. *Saint in the Wilderness*. Garden City, New York: Doubleday and Company, 1964.

Myers, Rawley. *People Who Loved*. Notre Dame: Fides, 1970.

Habig, M. A., O.F.M. *Saints of the Americas*. Huntington, Indiana: Our Sunday Visitor, 1974.

Learning Experience
Primary Level

TEACHER NOTES:

Dramatically relate the biographical information about Isaac Jogues and other North American Martyrs to the children, placing particular emphasis on their journey to the New World, their attempt to spread the Good News about Jesus to the Indians, and their experiences with the Indians after they arrived.

LEARNING EXPERIENCE: Indian Village

Provide the children with any materials that would assist them in creating a replica of one of the villages where Isaac Jogues lived and worked with his fellow Jesuits and the Indians in the North American Territory. Place several blankets, sheets, mats, or rugs in different places throughout the classroom on which the children may arrange their creations, and separate the children into groups of three or four to be responsible for various parts of the construction. Several youngsters may be assigned to create huts, others pathways and surrounding countryside, and others may wish to make pipe-cleaner figures to represent Father Jogues, his missionary companions and the Indian tribesmen he lived with. Give the children the opportunity to share what they have learned and created by inviting parents, other teachers and students into the classroom to comment on and question them about their work.

SUPPLIES:

Construction paper, scissors, paste, tape, sticks, pipe cleaners, sheets, blankets, mats for a base.

Learning Experience
Intermediate Level

TEACHER NOTES:

When you have related the biographical sketch about Isaac Jogues and the other North American Martyrs to the youngsters, bring them to a deeper appreciation of the courage and personal dedication required in the missionaries' day-to-day activities by first involving the youngsters in a discussion of the demands of their *own* daily schedule.

LEARNING EXPERIENCE: Daily Schedule of Activities

Ask the youngsters to jot down their actions on a typical day between nine in the morning and nine at night. Give them a few moments to talk about their favorite activities and their least liked ones—and then ask them to carry the paper with them and think seriously about the activities which were normally a part of the life of Isaac Jogues and his fellow missionaries.

Before they leave class ask them to select a particularly significant day from any of the many memorable ones described in the biography, and tell them to write down, throughout the day, the kinds of things the missionaries would have been involved in on that day.

When the youngsters have had time to share their work, invite them to complete a simple prayer expressing the feelings Isaac Jogues or one of the other martyrs may have had about his experiences on any one of the days of their life the youngsters explored.

Example: I praise you, dear Father, on this day because . . .

I ask that you please . . .

This day, Father, I thank you for . . .

I want you to know I love you because . . .

Learning Experience
Junior High Level

TEACHER NOTES:

When the students have had enough time to reflect on the information in the biography about Saint Isaac Jogues (or one of the other North American Martyrs), ask them to step inside his character for a few moments and examine what they believe motivated his actions.

LEARNING EXPERIENCE: Essay

Ask the students to describe Isaac Jogues (or one of the other North American Martyrs) in an essay, as if he were living today. Encourage the students to tell in their essays about the kind of clothes he might wear today, where he might live, the different kinds of people he might associate with, and the kind of job he might seek. They should include in their essay a brief explanation of the aspects of the missionaries' life which influenced their perception of the "modern-day saint" they envision. Ask them to note what impressed them most about the life-style of the real saint using as many events in his life as possible to illustrate their point. Invite the students to read carefully through one another's essays and perhaps vote on the one which best exemplifies the contemporary Isaac Jogues.

Kateri Tekakwitha (1656-1680)

"O great Spirit, whose voice I hear in the winds and whose breath gives life to all the world, hear me! . . . Make me wise so I may understand the things you have taught my people. Let me learn the lessons you have hidden in every leaf and rock. . . ."
— Red Cloud Indian School

There is a legend telling how the Huron refugee named Deganawidah and the Mohawk chief named Hiawatha founded, around the year 1570, the League of the Five Iroquois Tribes of New York. Their hope was that the League would bring about peace based on brotherhood among all the Indians. The League consisted of five Iroquois nations who lived in the northern part of New York: from east to west the Mohawks, Oneidas, Onondagas, Cayugas and Senecas. Representatives of all these tribes would convene every summer, usually at the principal town of the Onondagas.

The Iroquois tribes had always considered the French their enemies, and the French, from the beginning of Champlain's explorations, had always allied themselves with the Huron Nation, an ancient rival of the Iroquois. In 1648 the Iroquois finally conquered the Huron Nation and tortured to death the French missionaries who were living in their villages.

In 1656 the French attempted a trading and mission colony among the Onondaga Iroquois, but the settlement lasted only a year. For the next 10 years there was intermittent warfare between the Frenchmen and the five Iroquois nations, and then the French gathered together an army and marched into the territory of the Mohawks to subdue the League of the Five Nations. The League accepted defeat and sent emissaries to Quebec for the "burying of the war-club." One of the conditions of the peace agreement was to allow the presence of "blackrobes," or priests, in those Iroquois villages where there were Christian captives to be ministered to.

In 1668 the first Jesuit mission was established in the Iroquois Con-

19

federacy. Ten years later, 2,000 converts had been made, and among them was Kateri Tekakwitha of the Mohawks.

Kateri's father had been chief of the Turtle clan of the Mohawk tribe. Her mother was a Christian Algonquin, baptized by missionaries, who had lived among the French at Three Rivers until she had been taken captive to the village of Ossernenon. When Kateri was four years old she and her whole family caught smallpox during an epidemic; both parents and her younger brother died. Her aunt and uncle brought her to live with them in their longhouse and, though she recovered, she was left nearly blind and badly scarred. Her poor vision made it impossible for her to join freely in the games of the other young children, and it limited the kinds of work she was able to do as an adult.

Her character was "special" in many ways: she was very gentle and compassionate. She was horrified by the Iroquois custom of torturing captives publicly. She did not agree with the other Indians that this was a good opportunity for the captive to demonstrate his bravery.

As Kateri matured, her adoptive parents looked forward to her marriage because they would surely benefit when her husband moved into the longhouse with them and added his hunting and fighting skills to the family. But Kateri steadfastly refused marriage. Her aunt and uncle were puzzled and angered by this illogical position, and several young braves tried without success to persuade her to marry them.

When the Jesuits were allowed to enter the Iroquois villages in 1668 Kateri was almost 12 years old. She undoubtedly heard the Jesuits speaking with the Christian captives in the village, for often as many as 10 families lived in each of the longhouses and there was usually not much privacy. One day, when Kateri was unable to work because of her infirmity, Father Jacques de Lamberville sat with her and talked about Christ. She told him that she longed for Baptism and he immediately made plans for her instruction.

It was another affront to her adoptive parents when Kateri told them she wanted to be baptized. Apparently her uncle hated the blackrobes and their teachings, but he dared not oppose them openly because of the terms of the peace agreement. On April 5, 1676, when "the Lily of the Mohawks," as she was sometimes called, was 20 years old, Father Jacques de Lamberville baptized her, giving her the name Kateri or Catherine. This increased her uncle's irritation so much that the priest advised her to flee the village.

In the middle of July, 1676, she escaped to Caughnawaga, a village of Christian Indians located at Sault St. Louis near Montreal. There she found that she could live her faith openly. She received her First Communion on Christmas Day in 1676 — the first Iroquois to receive on Iroquois territory—and for the next three years led a life of austerity, charity, prayer and meditation. Although she was not a member of a religious order, on March 25, 1679, Kateri took a private vow of chastity. Her prayer life continued to grow and the next year, on April 17, she died at the age of 24.

In 1884, on the site in New York identified as the Mohawk village of Ossernenon, the Jesuits opened the National Shrine of the North American Martyrs. It commemorates the martyrdom of Saints Isaac Jogues, René Goupil and John LaLande. It is also the birthplace of Kateri Tekakwitha.

Recommended Readings

> Dollen, Charles. *Messengers to the Americas.* Collegeville, Minnesota: The Liturgical Press, 1975.
>
> Nevins, Albert J., M.M. *Our American Catholic Heritage.* Huntington, Indiana: Our Sunday Visitor, 1972.

Learning Experience
Primary Level

TEACHER NOTES:

Before relating the story of the life of Kateri Tekakwitha to the children, gather pictures from books, magazines, etc., of American Indians, particularly those found in the northeastern United States and Canada, to enrich your presentation. Refer from time to time to the photographs or illustrations in the materials you have compiled as you talk about Kateri in order to give the children a deeper appreciation of the environment in which she was raised and which later influenced the deepening of her Christian faith.

Involve the children in a discussion of her life by asking:

- What were her duties in the Indian village?
- How was she different from many other Indians of her tribe?
- How do you think Kateri felt when she saw prisoners being tortured in her camp?
- Who taught her about God's love for men?
- What was her life like in the Christian village?

LEARNING EXPERIENCE: Indian Headband

Provide the children with construction paper, scissors, crayons, magic markers, paste or tape, and invite each of them to make an Indian headband. Ask them to illustrate their headband with a picture showing one of the events in Kateri's life or to write on it one of the special things that they remember she did as a sign of her faith.

SUPPLIES:

Construction paper, scissors, crayons, magic markers, paste or tape.

Learning Experience
Intermediate Level

TEACHER NOTES:
After you have told Kateri Tekakwitha's story to the youngsters, capsulize the main events either on a blackboard or poster for them to refer to later on. It might be fun for the youngsters to elect a class historian each week who would be responsible for recording this type of information for the class.

LEARNING EXPERIENCE: Name-Letter Association Game
Supply the youngsters with paper, pencils or pens, and after a brief review to refresh their memories, ask them to print, vertically from the top to the bottom of their papers, the letters of Kateri's full name. Tell them to reflect on what they have learned about her for a few moments and then urge them to write, horizontally, next to each of the letters, a word which begins with the letter of her name and describes her in some way. Words which describe her personality, some of the people, or important events in her life would be most appropriate. Encourage the youngsters to share and compare their thoughts, and guide them in a discussion of the similarities and differences noted by the class, why they selected some of their words, and how the words and Kateri Tekakwitha's life are meaningful to them today.

SUPPLIES:
Paper, pencils.

Learning Experience
Junior High Level

TEACHER NOTES:
After the biographical sketch of Kateri Tekakwitha's life has been presented to the students, challenge them to express their thoughts about her life by writing a *cinquain.*

LEARNING EXPERIENCE: Cinquain
Explain to the students that a *cinquain,* derived from the French word for five (pronounced sin-can), is a poetic form composed of five lines.

- Line 1 — title (a noun, one word).
- Line 2 — description of the title (two words).
- Line 3 — action words or phrase about the title (three words).
- Line 4 — description of a feeling about the title (four words).
- Line 5 — reference to the title (one word).

Ask them to examine the following *cinquain* to see how it fits the description of the poetic form elaborated above.

> Christian
> Indian girl
> Enduring great suffering
> Always thankful for life
> Peace

When they have finished writing their poems, encourage the students to read one another's work and comment on their choice of words. Stimulate discussion in particular about how their poems would have compared or contrasted with the ones they have just created had their assignment been to write about the experiences of a contemporary Christian.

SUPPLIES:
Paper, pencils.

Jacques Marquette (1637-1675)

"Come, my friends, it is not too late to seek a newer world."
— Alfred Lord Tennyson

Adventures with explorers and fur traders! New missions in a strange land! Indian converts to the Catholic Faith! Sufferings, and even martyrdom!

In France, the periodical *Jesuit Relations* spread the news of the new French colonies growing in North America in the early 1600's. Explorers were traveling the waterways of the St. Lawrence River to find new rivers and tributaries which would lead them to more tribes of Indians, more land for France and more trading possibilities. Fur trade in beaver pelts brought much wealth to France, while missionaries accompanied the explorers and set up new mission posts along the way.

The missionaries reported their experiences as they worked to win converts among the Indians and wrote about their adjustments to the strange foods which they had to eat so they wouldn't insult the Indians. Although there were many difficult adjustments, especially cultural, they happily served God in spite of their many trials. Stories reporting the suffering, terrible tortures and martyrdom of the missionaries who fell into the hands of a particular hostile tribe brought tears to many eyes.

In Laon, France, young Jacques Marquette read about the ordeals of the missionaries in the *Jesuit Relations* and his adventurous spirit was kindled. He later became a Jesuit priest, with the intention of serving in the missions of North America. After ordination, his first assignment was at Three Rivers in Quebec, where he spent a year learning Indian customs and six difficult Indian dialects. In 1668 he was appointed to his first missionary post—among the Ottawa Indians at Chequamegon Bay on Lake Superior. He won the trust of the Indians with his works of charity, his sincerity, and his warm, outgoing personality.

With Father Claude Dablon, Marquette next traveled to the Ojibwas at the Sault to establish the Mission of Ste. Marie, the oldest mission in Michigan. They made their way by canoe across Lake Superior to Green Bay and the Fox River. Often their only food was pounded maize (corn) or moss from the rocks, and they were forced to wade in water or through snow with the cold biting into their bones and no fire to warm them. The possibility of captivity or death always loomed ahead of them.

With North American trade going so well, France was willing to protect the Indians who were her friends. On June 4, 1671, a congress of 14 Indian nations was called at the Mission of Ste. Marie and the French told the Indians about plans for their protection and for further exploration. A celebration which included hymns and the raising of a cedar cross closed the historical meeting. But later the same year the warring Sioux overpowered the mission. The peaceful Hurons fled with Father Marquette to the island of Mackinac in Lake Huron where the Mission of St. Ignace was established and where they had better protection.

In his talks with traveling Indians Marquette heard about the Missi Sepe (father of the waters) River and the Indian tales of the river monsters which attacked those who dared to trespass the waterway. Count de Frontenac, the Governor of New France, thought the river was the waterway to the Pacific through the Vermilion Sea (the Gulf of California). When Governor Frontenac commissioned the 27-year-old adventurer, fur trader and explorer, Louis Joliet, to explore the uncharted river, Marquette was invited to go, too. Delighted to have the chance to win converts and share this dream of discovery, he accepted.

In May, 1673, Marquette and Joliet paddled across Lake Michigan to Green Bay on the Fox River where the Wild Oats Indians lived. They were given this name because of the wild oats and rice which grew near their village. Marquette spoke to them in their native tongue: "My companion is an envoy of France to discover new countries; and I am ambassador from God to enlighten you with the gospel." He offered them presents and asked for two guides to help them on their trip. The guides were provided and a mat was given as a gift to Father Marquette for use in the canoe during his long trip. Before leaving, they all prayed for God's protection.

On June 10, 1673, Marquette, Joliet, five companion Frenchmen, and the two Algonquin guides carried their supplies and dragged the canoes to the Wisconsin River to begin their journey. The way was difficult and their moccasins were torn on the rocks, but their spirits remained high even when the guides deserted them.

They reached the Mississippi River on June 17 at what is now Prairie du Chien, Wisconsin. Day after day, on this expedition, they saw strange new plants, animals and tribes of Indians. About 180 miles from the Wisconsin River they saw footprints on the western bank of the Mississippi! Joliet and Marquette bravely resolved to meet what they expected this time to be savages. Six miles of walking brought them inland to a village of the Moingona (Des Moines) River and they became the first white men to set foot on Iowa soil. The "savages," to their surprise, were friendly "Illinois" Indians who warmly received them. An old chief cried out: "How beautiful is the sun, Frenchman, when you come to visit us! Our village awaits you;

enter in peace into our dwellings."

Marquette taught the Illinois about the true God, Manitou, who was their Creator and about the Canadian governor and the congress who wanted peace and offered protection. After six days of visiting, teaching and celebrating, the Illinois presented Marquette with a peace pipe (calumet) beautifully decorated with many colored bird feathers. This was to be Marquette's passport to peace as he met more new tribes on this voyage.

During their travels down the mighty Mississippi, they passed the noisy rushing waters of the Missouri River at what became St. Louis, Missouri, and later passed the Ohio River, whose banks were inhabited by the peaceful Shawnees. As they moved southward, the heat became unbearable and to protect themselves from the swarming mosquitoes they made awnings of sailcloth to cover the canoes. While on shore, they built scaffolds on which to sleep with smudge pots underneath. (They learned this mosquito deterrent from the Indians.) Farther along, they finally met the "river monsters" the Indians feared. The "monsters" which attacked their canoes were huge catfish!

From the western bank the Mitchigamea Indians saw the traveling party and armed themselves with bows and arrows, axes and clubs. With terrifying yells, they came out into the water in hollowed-out tree trunks to attack, but Father Marquette advised his companions to pray. He then held up the gift peace pipe for the attackers to see. At sight of the pipe, the attack suddenly became a welcome! They spoke through interpreters and Marquette again taught about the good news of the gospel and tried to win as many converts as possible.

Just below the entrance of the Arkansas River, Joliet and Marquette determined that the Mississippi flowed into the Gulf of Mexico and not the Gulf of California as the Governor thought. They had no reason to go farther. The travelers had been told to expect hostile tribes farther south, and they were afraid that, if captured, their carefully kept charts and journals would be destroyed and France would not benefit from the information they had gathered.

As they returned by way of the Illinois River, peaceful prairies lay before them abounding with buffalo, deer, beaver and other game.

> Joliet wrote: "When I was told of a country without trees, I imagined a country that had been burned over, or of a soil too poor to produce anything; but we have remarked just the contrary, and it would be impossible to find a better soil for grain, for vines, or any fruits whatever. . . . There is no need that an emigrant should employ ten years in cutting down the forest and burning it. On the day of his arrival the emigrant could put the plough into the earth."

In very poor health from his ordeal on the Mississippi, Father Marquette returned to the Illinois tribe to recover. He taught them more about God and about Mary for whom he had great devotion and celebrated Easter Mass with them in 1675.

Still very ill, Father Marquette left the Illinois tribe to return to Mackinac. On the way, he believed he would soon die, so he asked to be put on shore to pray. He blessed his fellow travelers and peacefully passed away near Ludington, Michigan, on May 18, 1675, at the age of 38. His companions sorrowfully buried him on a grassy knoll by the riverside. (The site where he died is commemorated by a plaque at Damen Avenue and the north end of the bridge over the Chicago River.) Father Marquette never returned to his beloved Mackinac.

After Joliet had transcribed his notes into a full account of the trip, he set out to deliver the narrative to Governor Frontenac in Quebec. During a sudden storm his charts and records were lost, but he later rewrote much from memory with Father Dablon's assistance. As a result of Joliet's notes, Robert Cavelier de la Salle traveled the Mississippi all the way to the Gulf of Mexico and raised a cross in honor of God and France in 1682. He erected a stone which claimed that all the land bordering the Mississippi River belonged to France and named it Louisiana in honor of the French king, Louis XIV. (Many years later, the French would lose some of these territories to England.)

In history books, Jacques Marquette is most often noted for the exploration of the Mississippi River. Because of his ability to relate well to the Indians and to speak six Indian languages fluently, he was called upon to accompany Joliet on the 2,500-mile exploratory trip, mostly by canoe. He was primarily dedicated to sharing his own love of God with the Indians and treating them with brotherly love and respect so they would come to know God, too.

In grand tribute, the Jesuits named Marquette University in Milwaukee, Wisconsin, in his honor. A statue of Marquette, representing the state of Wisconsin, stands in the Hall of Fame in the Capitol Building, Washington, D.C. A plaque at the base of the statue is proudly inscribed, "JAMES MARQUETTE, S.J. WHO WITH LOUIS JOLLIET (sic) DISCOVERED THE MISSISSIPPI RIVER AT PRAIRIE du CHIEN, WISCONSIN JUNE 17, 1673." Though born in France, he lived most of his life and died in America, serving both God and country.

Recommended Readings

Donnelly, Joseph P. *Jacques Marquette, S.J., 1637-1675*. Chicago: Loyola University Press, 1968.

Hamilton, Raphael. *Marquette's Explorations: The Narratives Reexamined*. Madison, Wisconsin: University of Wisconsin Press, 1970.

Learning Experience
Primary Level

TEACHER NOTES:

After telling the story of Jacques Marquette's life to the children, take a few moments to talk with them about: the things that he did which they thought were most exciting, the adventures they thought were most frightening, or perhaps the happiest moments in his life.

LEARNING EXPERIENCE: TV Show

When the children have had time to recall and comment on the different phases of Father Marquette's eventful life, and when you have a definite idea of what aspects of his life impressed them most, challenge the class to create a "TV Show" about him.

Separate the class into four or five groups, distribute long pieces of shelf or mural paper to each group and assign each group a sequence, characteristic, or highlight of Father Marquette's life to illustrate. Ask them to color or paint their drawings and when each group has finished, attach the different segments of the "TV Show" together with clear tape. Using an appropriately sized box (as determined by the width of the paper) as viewer or a "TV set," have each group select a narrator to explain the pictures in their segment and stage the show for the whole class. Be sure to give "credit" to all the children who helped in creating the production by including their names on an additional sheet of paper attached at the end . . . "with special thanks to Jacques Marquette!"

SUPPLIES:

Roll of shelf or mural paper, cardboard box, pens, pencils, crayons, magic markers or tempera paints, clear tape.

Learning Experience
Intermediate Level

TEACHER NOTES:

When the youngsters have had time to reflect on the biography of Jacques Marquette, stimulate discussion among them about the feelings, expectations, reactions, reservations he may have had concerning his missionary work by asking questions such as:

- What thoughts do you think ran through Father Marquette's mind when he was journeying for the first time across the ocean to New France?
- Why did Father Marquette want to learn the Indians' languages and customs?
- Why did he want to travel down the Mississippi with Joliet?

LEARNING EXPERIENCE: Diary

Pass out paper and pencils to the youngsters and tell them to write about an experience of Jacques Marquette as they would imagine he himself would actually have related his thoughts in his extensive diary. Tell them to select any event of his life referred to in the biography and remind them that because there was no other method of communication, Marquette probably had hoped that his diaries would be sent to France to inspire others to come to this country to live and serve God.

SUPPLIES:

Paper, pencils, pens.

Learning Experience
Junior High Level

TEACHER NOTES:

After reviewing the material in the biography on Jacques Marquette with the students, discuss with them, for a brief period, the many facets of our American experience of traveling throughout the country today, i.e., various modes of transportation available, cost, travel time, reasons why people travel, comforts and discomforts associated with the different methods of travel, etc. To bring them to appreciation of the difficulties Jacques Marquette and his fellow missionaries had to cope with on the frontier, focus their attention on transportation in the 17th century.

LEARNING EXPERIENCE: Wilderness Travel Agency

Provide the students with a variety of materials and tell them to set up a "travel agency" complete with travel posters, maps, travel folders and information on accommodations, foods, climate, language and customs of the "native" Americans that would be of service to the "wilderness traveler" pioneering through the heartland of America in Jacques Marquette's day. Encourage the students to use encyclopedias, almanacs, travel magazines and even local travel agencies as resources for their information but ask them to create original illustrations and data whenever possible to simulate authentic frontier conditions. Outdated road maps, usually available in local service stations, could be worked over with magic marker to map out a particular route a traveler might take and may also be used as a backdrop for a "billboard" (set up on a bulletin board in the classroom) to advertise and inspire wilderness travelers.

SUPPLIES:

Paper, pens, poster paper, magic markers, old road maps, old magazines.

Junipero Serra (1713-1784)
and New Spain

"Lord, make me an instrument of your peace. . . . Where there is hatred, let me sow love . . . where there is doubt, faith; where there is despair, hope . . . and where there is sadness, joy. . . ."
— Prayer of Saint Francis

After Columbus claimed the land he called San Salvador for Spain, the Spanish thrust of "glory, God and gold" caused the establishment of many small fringe colonies and trading posts in the West Indies. Mexico was discovered in 1517 and Cortes' conquest took place in 1519-1521. By 1600, the quest for gold had led Spain to conquer almost the whole of coastal South America except Brazil and much of the interior as well.

As early as the 1520's Spanish missionaries were busy converting the Indians in New Spain to Christianity. Countless numbers were baptized as these dedicated priests even pushed ahead of adventurers, explorers and settlers.

One of the outstanding names in the development of New Spain is Bartolme de las Casas (1474-1566). This Spanish Dominican missionary and bishop, a former colonizer himself and a compassionate man, was an early pioneer in upholding the Indians' human rights. He was instrumental in

33

the development of the New Laws of 1542-43, which among other things prohibited Indian slavery and decreed new regulations for discoveries and conquests.

The Jesuit Eusebio Kino (1645-1711) was the first to bring Christianity and Spanish civilization successfully to southern Arizona and lower California. He lived among the Pima Indians from 1687 until his death in 1711. His maps were the first to show that California was not an island. More than 100 years later, the French-born Archbishop John Lamy (1840-1888), the inspiration of Willa Cather's *Death Comes for the Archbishop* (New York: Knopf, 1927), labored mainly in New Mexico and built firm foundations in education and parish administration.

California, as we know it, was not colonized until 1769 when Spain had only half a century left in North America. It might not have happened even then but the Spanish Ambassador at Moscow heard that the Russians were interested in California and were readying ships and settlers. When he passed along this news, José de Galvez, visitor-general to Mexico City on behalf of the crown, responded by commissioning the colonization of Upper California.

What would cause a person to want to be part of that effort? Some of the attractions are characterized in this "want ad" from the mythical *New Spain Gazette:*

> HELP WANTED: MISSION BUILDER & DEVELOPER
> New opening for creative, resourceful, mature person of faith with instincts of a missionary who welcomes challenge, likes people and thinks ahead.
>
> This is a position that requires intelligence and congeniality. You will be constantly meeting the public; you will need to be open-minded and flexible, and you must be ready to meet predictable and unpredictable needs and desires.
>
> If you qualify, contact—in person—
> José de Galvez
> Imperial Inspector, Mexico City

The two leaders of the Northern California settlement party were Captain Gaspar de Portola, appointed governor of the province, and Padre Junipero Serra, a Franciscan missionary. Serra had been in Mexico since 1749 teaching in the San Fernando missionary college in Mexico City and working among the Pame Indians, building new churches and supervising others. He had a reputation as a good and holy man.

Born in Majorca, Spain, on November 24, 1713, José Miguel Serra grew up on his parents' farm and entered the Franciscans when he was 17, taking the name Junipero. A brilliant man and an accomplished scholar, he was a professor of philosophy at the Lullian University for 15 years. He was well known for his oratory.

When he was 36, Serra asked to go to the missions in Mexico and his friend, Father Francisco Palou, went with him. Palou kept a record of their work and later wrote Serra's biography, *La Vida de Junipero Serra* (Ann Arbor, Michigan: University Microfilm, 1966). It is currently available in many local libraries.

Many legends tell of Junipero Serra walking from mission to mission, but it was only in Mexico that walking was his usual method of transportation. In Upper California he rode a mule or a horse accompanied by a military guard.

Though he suffered from many physical problems—ulcerated feet and legs as well as asthma—Serra is generally characterized as a short, stocky man with rosy cheeks, a quick smile and sparkling eyes. Yet we know from his work that he struggled with many very real problems — unfamiliar territory, fearsome Indians, inadequate supplies, carelessness and indifference of government officials. Letters reveal the serious side of this gentle and extraordinarily capable man.

> As regards our food supply . . . I intended to say a great deal, but will limit myself to this that our sufferings are great; never have we, the religious, been in such dire straits. . . . It would be most helpful if Your Excellency were to give strict orders to the Commissary at San Blas, that he take greater care than he has till now taken in the packing of provisions forwarded for the maintenance of these missions. . . . If the corn is put on board when it has already been attacked by grubs, what will be its state when it arrives at its destination and what condition will it be in when the time comes to eat it? . . . Last year there was no meat; and this year, our meat supply was neither much, nor little, but nil. . . . The greatest pity of all has been concerning the flour, which is, of all the things that are sent us, or may be sent, the most helpful and most basic for the sustenance of life. It was put in plain sacks of poor material made of burlap or hemp, and consequently ran out at every motion or contact; and so the assignments arrived minus much that should have been there. . . .
>
> —*excerpt from Serra's* "Report on the general condition and needs of the missions of Upper California" *prepared for the Viceroy, Antonio Maria de Bucareli y Ursua, dated March 13, 1773.**

*From Antonine Tibesar, ed., *Writings of Junipero Serra.* Washington, D.C., 1955. Volume I, pages 295-327.

At the time Serra wrote this letter he had established and supervised the building of five missions — San Diego (1769), San Carlos Borromeo (1770), San Antonio (1771), San Gabriel (1771), San Luis Obispo (1772). Before his death he founded four more missions in Upper California — San Francisco (1776), San Juan Capistrano (1776), Santa Clara (1777), and San Buenaventura (1782). These nine important missions and the 12 more that his successors founded were the beginnings of California's great cities and the keys to the colonization and development of that part of New Spain.

Each mission was begun in the same way. First a cross was erected and a church bell was hung signaling the beginning of a little chapel in the wilderness. In the Spanish mission system — by which it was thought the Indians would learn all the advantages of "civilization" — the first task was to build trust between the missionaries and the local Indians. Then the Indians were invited to live and work at the mission, where they were taught Spanish methods of farming and of raising sheep and cattle. Catechisms, many times written by the missionaries themselves, contained teaching on faith, moral living, prayers and also often covered planting, irrigation, harvesting, and the rotation of crops as well as other practical subjects.

Usually there would be a village attached to the mission quadrangle. Those who did not live in the village would stay in the quadrangle which contained the workshops and the dormitories. In the workshops many skills and crafts were taught.

The missions served as educational, religious and social centers and at times they served defense purposes as well. As each expanded its work and as the village attached to it became self-sufficient, it was time to start a new mission. A day's trip, usually about 30 miles, would bring missionaries like Serra to the edge of the wilderness where a cross would be erected, a church bell hung and the same slow process begun all over again.

Often there was a wide gap between the noble intention of converting the Indians and the actual brutality that the Spanish adopted in response to their greed. Serra was a staunch supporter of the Indians' human rights and vigorously defended them against Spanish abuses.

He died at the Carmel Mission on August 28, 1784 — 15 years after the colonization of California had begun. Yet, much of the Spanish heritage evident in California and throughout the Southwest today is credited to the work of Junipero Serra and the other missionaries who shared his vision. Congress created Statuary Hall in 1864 and invited each state to send for display two marble or bronze statues of citizens who had performed distinguished services. California honored Serra by presenting his statue in 1931.

Recommended Readings

Geiger, Maynard. *Franciscan Missionaries in Hispanic California: 1769-1848*. San Marino, California: Huntington Library, 1969.

Sullivan, Marion Frances. *Westward the Bells*. New York: Alba House, 1971.

Wise, Winifred F. *Fray Junipero Serra and the California Conquest*. New York: Scribner's, 1967.

Learning Experience
Primary Level

TEACHER NOTES:

As you relate the story of Junipero Serra's life to the children, use a map or globe to point out the many miles Serra traveled during his lifetime. Show them also approximately where Father Serra established his missions and draw their attention to the fact that great American cities grew around the very missions Junipero Serra founded. Focus their attention on his life-style as a Franciscan priest, and explain to the children that he belonged to a religious community which promised to live very simply, with very few possessions, devoting itself to the service of God. Tell them that he personally felt he could best serve God by going to California to teach the Indians there about God's love for them. Mention that as he traveled through the territory together with the Indians, he founded places where they all could live, learn and pray together, called *missions*. Explain that the missions were usually made up of several buildings, a school, and dwellings, clustered together near or around a church. Note that somewhere within the mission there were bells that were used to call the different members of the community together from the surrounding fields and schools for meals and the celebration of Mass.

LEARNING EXPERIENCE: "Mission" Construction

Gather together a collection of boxes in all sizes and shapes (from your local grocery store), tempera paint and magic markers, and ask the children to paint and arrange the boxes to resemble one of the missions where Father Serra lived and worked. When they have completed their task, the children may enjoy the experience of moving throughout their construction and role-playing Junipero Serra's activities within his mission community.

SUPPLIES:

Boxes, tempera paint, black magic markers.

Learning Experience
Intermediate Level

TEACHER NOTES:
While you are telling the story of Junipero Serra's life, it would be helpful if you utilized a class "historian" or recorded on the blackboard or on poster paper the major events, significant people and places in his life.

LEARNING EXPERIENCE: Footprints
Begin your learning experience by separating the youngsters in your class into groups of two or three. Tell each group they will be responsible for printing with magic markers certain specific facts and important data on large precut footprints you have prepared beforehand from sturdy poster paper or contact paper. (The footprints should be at least three feet long and approximately two feet wide.) After the youngsters have recorded the information assigned to them, affix the "footprints" to the floor at various spots throughout the classroom. Invite them to explore and become familiar with the experiences of Junipero Serra as they follow the trail of his footsteps and adventures while a missionary 200 years ago in California.

SUPPLIES:
Sturdy poster or contact paper "footprints," magic markers, adhesive.

Learning Experience
Junior High Level

TEACHER NOTES:
After they have fully explored the data from the biography of Junipero Serra, challenge the students to examine a word maze containing names, places and significant words expressing his life and times. (An example of a word maze pertaining to the life of Junipero Serra is included below. It may be duplicated or you may wish to devise one for the students yourself.)

LEARNING EXPERIENCE: Word Maze
Ask students to identify and circle the words that they find in the maze which are pertinent to the life of Father Serra and question them as to what aspect of his life the words describe. Offer them an opportunity to deepen their appreciation of Father Serra's extraordinary life by inviting them to create a word maze containing words which meaningfully describe their own lives.

Word Maze:

```
C  H  R  I  S  T  J  O  Y  M  E  X  I  C  O  S
Z  F  R  A  N  C  I  S  C  O  P  A  L  O  U  A
K  M  L  X  R  A  K  M  L  R  O  M  D  N  P  N
M  O  V  E  N  P  I  I  A  Q  L  R  N  F  C  G
T  E  A  C  H  I  N  S  H  J  P  Y  U  I  I  A
R  K  S  Q  S  S  D  S  W  A  O  A  D  R  V  B
C  H  A  R  I  T  Y  I  S  O  R  R  M  M  N  R
I  T  N  C  A  R  L  O  S  S  R  D  C  P  X  I
N  B  D  P  O  A  Z  N  S  P  T  K  Z  A  W  E
D  S  A  N  A  N  N  A  B  A  P  T  I  Z  E  L
I  D  I  E  G  O  P  R  G  I  Y  A  M  E  L  K
A  H  U  M  B  L  E  Y  B  N  A  R  N  A  O  I
N  J  O  S  E  D  E  G  A  L  V  E  Z  L  V  N
S  A  N  F  R  A  N  C  I  S  C  O  X  P  E  O
```

Look for these words:

Majorca	Charity	Love
Hard Work	San Carlos	Baptize
Kind	Capistrano	Spain
Confirm	Missionary	Teach
Francisco Palou	San Diego	Christ
Indians	Humble	Joy
San Gabriel	Jose de Galvez	Mexico
Kino	San Francisco	Zeal

Paraliturgical Celebration for Unit I
Era of Exploration and Colonization

Theme:

Isaac Jogues, Jacques Marquette, Kateri Tekakwitha and Junipero Serra have gone before us to tell the early inhabitants of our country about their Father, a loving God who sent his Son to be our Savior. Today let us reflect on the suffering and deep commitment of these holy people. Let us celebrate the joy they felt as those early people began to call that loving God, "our Father," and his Savior Son, "our Brother."

Entrance Hymn:

"Men of Faith," Carey Landry, *Songs of Praise and Reconciliation,* N.A.L.R.; "If I Had a Hammer," Pete Seeger and Lee Hayes, *American Favorite Ballads,* Oak Publications; "O God Our Help in Ages Past," Wesley, *Worship,* G.I.A.

Penitential Rite:

For the times when because of the color of a person's skin, or their language, or ethnic background, we have not offered to share their joys or sorrows, Lord, have mercy.

LORD, HAVE MERCY.

For the many times we have complained about our own pain and discomfort, Christ, have mercy.

CHRIST, HAVE MERCY.

For failing to recognize and share with others our gifts of wisdom, understanding, fortitude and hope, Lord, have mercy.

LORD, HAVE MERCY.

First Reading:

(John 17: 20-26)

Gospel Reading:

(Matthew 28: 16-20)

Homily:

Comment on the faith of these extraordinary Catholic Americans whose lives the youngsters have explored and together with the passage from John in the First Reading, help them to reflect on and become more sensitive to their own unique mission as disciples of Christ in our world today.

Song:

"O Lord Make Us Ready," Tom Parker, *People's Mass Book,* W.L.P.; "All Good Gifts," Stephen Schwartz, *Godspell,* Celebration Services Ltd.; "Come Before the Table of the Lord," Tom Parker, *People's Mass Book,* W.L.P.; "Whatsoever You Do," Jabusch, *Worship,* G.I.A.; "I Wonder Why," *No Time Like the Present,* W.L.P.; "Let Us Break Bread Together," traditional, *Worship,* G.I.A.

Meditation:

While a small group of youngsters from the class sings, "Happy the Man," show a series of slides appropriately depicting the faith and service of the Catholic Americans the youngsters have studied. Include in the series slides of helping hands, people praying, perhaps even slides showing forests typical of the northwest, rivers, valleys and hills similar to those found in California.

Recessional:

"Sent Forth By God's Blessing," *People's Mass Book,* W.L.P.; "You Fill the Day," Joe Wise, *People's Mass Book,* W.L.P.; "A Mighty Fortress Is Our God," Luther, *Worship,* G.I.A.

Note:

Use as much of the work developed in the original learning experience as possible in the liturgy. Some youngsters may carry appropriate artwork, etc., in the entrance procession and recessional.

UNIT II

Shaping a Nation

The Carrolls (John Carroll: 1735-1815)

"Liberty in All Things!"
— Carroll Family Motto

What is it like to be popular and unpopular; respected, yet imprisoned; the victim of a wrecked career, yet a tremendous success; quiet, yet outspoken for rights and religious freedom?

A giant of a man emerged from the mold of these ingredients, and John Carroll was that man. To know him, though, it is helpful to know about his family, the aristocratic Carrolls of Maryland. They stand out among those who laid the foundations of our government.

Daniel Carroll, John's older brother, served in the state and national government for 18 years at various levels. He fought for religious freedom and was a loyal patriot. He served in the Constitutional Convention and was among the signers of the United States Constitution. As Planning Commissioner for the capitol in Washington, D.C., he donated one of his own farms for the site. (At that time, Washington, D.C., was part of Maryland.) He helped George Washington organize the Revolutionary Army and donated his own money for supplies.

Charles Carroll, John's cousin, was the wealthiest man in the United States, and also prominent in government. He spoke out against unfair British taxation in a series of letters published in the *Maryland Gazette* in 1773, signing his name only as "First Citizen." In his letter debates with "Second Citizen," who was loyal to the British throne, Charles supported the rights of the colonists. When the community learned Charles was "First Citizen" they publicly thanked him for defending their rights. Charles showed it was possible to be a good citizen *and* a good Catholic at the same time.

During this time it was unlawful for Catholics to practice their faith publicly, to have schools, to hold public office, or even to vote. (When Charles' grandfather came to Maryland there was freedom of worship for everyone, according to the Toleration Act of 1649. The Act was repealed in 1654 and it was not until 1776 that religious freedom was again declared by Maryland.) But Charles, though a Catholic, was accepted by the officials because of his "First Citizen" letters and his aristocratic social position. During his lifetime, Charles served the Continental Congress, was both Congressman and the first Senator of Maryland, served on the "Board of War" and protected George Washington from a conspiracy to take over his army.

At great personal risk Charles signed the Declaration of Independence and was the *only* Catholic to do so. He also voted for the First Amendment to the Constitution, which granted religious freedom to all persons in America. The ratification of this amendment was one of the happiest days of his life.

Charles served so well that, in 1778, he was asked by the Federalists to serve as the second President of the United States. The Federalists believed that a strong central government would insure unity in the new nation. Rather than accept the presidency, Charles chose to retire from the U.S. Senate and to return to the Maryland Senate. Much later, he was the director of commercial companies to encourage westward expansion. As a "grand old man" of 91 years, he laid the cornerstone of the new Baltimore and Ohio Railroad, July 4, 1828. This was an overland route, previously undreamt of, all the way to the Ohio River! He died at age 95 as the longest survivor of the signers of the Declaration of Independence.

John Carroll, affectionately called "Jacky," was educated in the "illegal" Catholic Jesuit school, Bohemia Manor, and the Jesuit college of St. Omer in France. The school was "illegal" because the law decreed that Catholics could not operate schools. But the officials did not take any action to close the school because they were busy with other more serious problems. Following the example of the courageous Jesuit priests in their work and in the schools, John became a Jesuit priest. As a respected scholar, he taught in the Jesuit college at Liège, France, and toured central and southern Europe as a tutor.

But on July 21, 1773, his religious order, the Society of Jesus, was disbanded by papal order. So far, this was the low point of his life. As a young man he had been secure in wealth and social position, and then had entered a distinguished religious order and achieved a stable and highly respected teaching position. Now he was suddenly jobless and transferred to the position of a secular priest at 39 years of age. What would he do next?

He did not know that his decision would shape the history of the Church in North America. Temporarily, he served as a family chaplain in England, but in spring, 1774, he chose to return to his mother's home in Rock Creek, Maryland. Instead of living a quiet life of seclusion to "lick his wounds," he traveled by horseback to the surrounding areas, quietly but zealously fulfilling his priestly duties. Father Carroll administered the sacraments and cared for the needs of the Catholics scattered through the countryside. On the grounds of his mother's home a chapel was built where Mass could be celebrated. In his travels, Father Carroll celebrated Mass both in private manor homes and in servant shanties.

These were troubled times for the colonists. They felt they were entitled to freedom and respect for their rights, but none really wanted war. John sided with the patriots who were having problems with England and were struggling for independence. Because of the American situation, he personally refused to submit to the authority of the pope's Vicar General in England. Nevertheless, in his whole lifetime, John remained fiercely loyal to Rome.

As a dynamic young priest who assumed leadership casually, he met with all the priests of his disbanded order (then about 25) to help organize them and also to form a trusteeship to protect all the order's properties. A trusteeship put the land in the hands of groups of laymen. This trusteeism later proved unpopular with several priests because some of the lay groups, against the bishop's request, tried to hire and fire the priests of their choice.

Because he was a loyal citizen, a priest, and because he spoke fluent French and might be an influence with Canadian Bishop Briand, John was asked by the new Continental Congress in 1776 to accompany his cousin Charles, Samuel Chase and Benjamin Franklin to Montreal in order to seek Canada's help against England. John was very reluctant because he felt that priests shouldn't become involved in politics. Finally, after much persuasion, he agreed to go. The mission failed, however, and Canada remained neutral until the outbreak of the Revolutionary War.

John then accompanied the discouraged and ailing Franklin on his return to Philadelphia and took care of him. A bond of friendship developed between the two leaders, and nine years later Dr. Franklin recommended to the pope that John would make a good candidate "to be made head of the missions in the United States."

Rome studied the matter and notified John of his assignment on June 9, 1784. Father Carroll understood the burdens of being Apostolic Prefect and preferred not to accept the position. Instead, he chose to let the priests vote on their choice of leader. The only vote cast against him was his own, and he accepted his new responsibility graciously. In addition to reporting to Rome about the status of the "mission lands," he organized the Church and continually defended the rights of the American Catholics.

On September 17, 1789, Pope Pius VI formally appointed John the *first* bishop of the *first* diocese in America with the "See" (headquarters) in Baltimore. Bishop Carroll was consecrated in Dorset, England, on August 15, 1790. In 1791, he called the first National Synod of Priests to discuss, among other topics, the guidelines for the administration of the sacraments to the Catholic minority. (Several years later, in 1808, Bishop Carroll became archbishop and Baltimore became an archdiocese. At his request, four other dioceses were formed—in Boston, Philadelphia, New York and Bardstown, Kentucky.)

After George Washington was inaugurated as President at Federal Hall in New York, April 30, 1789, John Carroll wrote an "Address of the Roman Catholics to the President." He warmly congratulated George Washington on his election as president and affirmed that Catholics had rights to justice and equality. President Washington agreed wholeheartedly and replied that as men grew more liberal, equal rights would be had by all. It was his firm belief that America should be foremost among nations of the world in having equal rights. President Washington also said,

> And I presume that your fellow citizens will not forget the patriotic part which you took in the accomplishment of their Revolution, and the establishment of their government; nor the important assistance which they received from a nation in which the Roman Catholic religion is professed.

Bishop Carroll visited his good friend, George Washington, often during his retirement after his presidency.

Throughout his service to the Church, John upheld democratic and just procedures which were true to the American ideals. The American Catholic Church differed from the European Catholic Church in one important factor—Church and state were separate. This was a Church formed to fit America's needs. Bishop Carroll was the first to establish public prayers for officials in public office. He also requested Rome to allow the Mass to be prayed in the vernacular so that average people who were unschooled in Latin could understand what they were praying. Rome said "no" and unfortunately his revolutionary idea did not become a reality until Vatican II. Bishop Carroll, however, did succeed in adapting new guidelines for the administration of the sacraments in America.

In cooperation with the government, as the colonists and the new immigrants moved westward, Bishop Carroll was careful to assign priests who were good priests *and* good citizens.

An educational system was set up, including a seminary in Baltimore to form priests; Georgetown (which is now Georgetown University in Washington, D.C.), Mount St. Mary's College and St. Joseph and Visitation Academies for girls. He felt that religious education was vital for the growth of the Church and he encouraged Elizabeth Seton, a convert (see biography), to begin a free parochial school system. Bishop Carroll brought in many religious orders to help with the mission work in America. Among them were Augustinians, Dominicans, Sulpicians, Visitation nuns, Sisters of Charity, Sisters of Loretto, Carmelites and Poor Clares.

To assist in the growth of the Church, he also encouraged lay assistance and lay councils. Ecumenical ahead of his time, he was president of the Board of Trustees for the all-denominational Baltimore College. He was elected Provost to the University of Maryland in 1812, but at age 77 could not accept because of his many other pressing duties!

Although the then Archbishop Carroll did not live to see its completion, he planned the Cathedral of the Assumption with architect Benjamin Latrobe in Baltimore. He died on December 3, 1815, at age 80. Thousands of sorrowing people paid tribute to this great man: Catholics, Protestants, Jews, blacks, whites, great dignitaries and humble servants. His remains were later moved from St. Mary's Seminary Chapel to the cathedral.

Throughout his whole life, John Carroll was amiable, gentle, good-humored, polished, dignified and a good conversationalist who put everyone at ease. He respected the American ideals, fought for them, lived them and he shaped the Catholic Church in America. He saw religious freedom come to America in the Virginia and Maryland Toleration Acts and the ratification of the First Amendment. In 1806, his old Jesuit order was restored in the States and the Jesuits began work on his pet project, Georgetown College. He could only have felt as his life ended, "Lord, I served you in every way possible."

Today, John Carroll University, outside Cleveland, Ohio, stands as a monument to this spiritual father of our country.

Recommended Readings

Guilding, Peter. *The Life and Times of John Carroll, Archbishop of Baltimore: 1735-1815.* New York: Newman, 1954.

Melville, Annabelle (McConnell). *John Carroll of Baltimore, Founder of the American Hierarchy.* New York: Scribner's, 1955.

Learning Experience
Primary Level

TEACHER NOTES:

When the children have become familiar with the biography of John Carroll, discuss with them his role as "Good Shepherd" to the flock of early

American Catholics. Tell the children that he labored to provide religious freedom and education for Catholics in his time, and that he wore a hat called a "mitre" and carried a "staff" as symbols of his office on special occasions. Explain that even today bishops still wear a mitre and carry the staff as signs of their service to our worshiping communities. Compare these symbols to those associated with other helping, caring people (policemen, firemen, priests, teachers, nurses, etc.), who live and work in their neighborhoods.

LEARNING EXPERIENCE: Bishop's Mitre and Staff

If possible have a "mitre" and "staff" already constructed for the children to examine and then pass out materials and invite them to make one or both. For the mitre pass out scissors, construction paper, paste and crayons and ask the children to draw pictures on the front and back of the mitre before they assemble it to remind them of Bishop Carroll's life. Have the children cut the staff from stiff cardboard or construction paper, making it about two inches in width so that they may draw and color symbols from Bishop Carroll's life on it as well.

SUPPLIES:

Scissors, construction paper, stiff cardboard, paste, crayons.

Learning Experience
Intermediate Level

TEACHER NOTES:

Before the youngsters begin to explore the life of John Carroll through the following learning experience, it would be helpful if they could review the biography again, either by reading it over or by listening to a recording of it at a learning center in the classroom.

LEARNING EXPERIENCE: Tic-Tac-Toe Game

Divide the class into groups of five, each group having two teams of two "players" each and one "judge." Decide which team will go first and provide the "judge" with an answer key.

The first "player" picks any square and answers either of the questions in the square. If the "judge" accepts the answer, an "X" or an "O" is placed in the square. If the "judge" says the answer is wrong, a line is drawn through that question but the other question in the square remains available for play.

SUPPLIES:

Tic-Tac-Toe Game and answer key as outlined on the following pages.

Tic-Tac-Toe Game:

1a John Carroll was educated at .... in Maryland.

1b John Carroll cared for .... when he became ill on a return trip to Philadelphia.

2a True or False: "The Address of the Roman Catholics to the President" was an angry message demanding rights for Catholics.

2b True or False: Canada was happy to help the Americans fight the English in 1775.

3a The famous .... in Washington, D.C., was founded by Bishop John Carroll.

3b John Carroll's cousin .... was the only Catholic to sign the Declaration of Independence.

4a Bishop Carroll encouraged .... to start free parochial schools in Maryland.

4b The Continental Congress voted for the ...., in 1776.

5a The first Bishop in the United States was ....

5b In France, John Carroll attended the Jesuit college, ...

6a As a boy John Carroll's nickname was ....

6b "First Citizen" was the name signed by ...., in the *Maryland Gazette*.

7a The First Amendment of the Constitution provides the ....

7b Name two "rights" which Catholics were denied before 1776.

8a John Carroll's brother .... signed the United States Constitution.

8b The Cathedral of the .... was planned by Archbishop Carroll.

9a John Carroll was consecrated as a Bishop in .... on Aug. 15, 1790.

9b The first Catholic diocese in the United States was located in ....,

Answer Key for Tic-Tac-Toe Game:

1a.   Bohemia Manor
1b.   Benjamin Franklin
2a.   False
2b.   False
3a.   Georgetown University
3b.   Charles
4a.   Elizabeth Seton
4b.   Declaration of Independence
5a.   John Carroll
5b.   St. Omer
6a.   "Jacky"
6b.   Charles Carroll
7a.   The right of all citizens to have freedom to practice the religion of their choice.
7b.   The right to have schools, the right to hold public office, the right to worship publicly and the right to vote (any two of the four for a correct answer).
8a.   Daniel
8b.   Assumption
9a.   England
9b.   Baltimore, Maryland

Learning Experience
Junior High Level

TEACHER NOTES:

Give the students time to reflect on the biography of John Carroll, separate them into groups and then challenge each group to decide on the four greatest accomplishments of John Carroll's life. When each group has come to a consensus, focus their attention on how the accomplishments they have selected as most significant reflect John Carroll's lifelong dedication to establish and preserve the American Catholic's right freely and meaningfully to express his faith.

LEARNING EXPERIENCE: Shield/Coat of Arms

Supply each group with poster board and magic markers and invite them to make a shield as a sign of John Carroll's efforts as a defender of religious liberty. Tell them to come up with symbols of the accomplishments they decided on earlier as his "greatest" and to arrange them in a composite coat of arms to decorate the shield.

SUPPLIES:

Poster board, scissors, magic markers.

Elizabeth Seton (1774-1821)

"The response to the divine call may come at any age . . . the years do not count before God, but rather the intensity of the love with which one answers him."

— Pope John XXIII

Elizabeth Bayley was born into a prominent colonial family in New York City on August 28, 1774, two years before the Declaration of Independence was signed. Her mother, the daughter of an Anglican clergyman who was the rector of Saint Andrews Church, Staten Island, died when Elizabeth was three. Her father, a Loyalist and a distinguished surgeon, was the first professor of anatomy at King's College, now Columbia University. He was later named Inspector General of the New York Public Health Service.

Elizabeth's early life, between the ages of two and nine, coincided with the years of the Revolutionary War. "Redcoats" along the cobblestone streets were a familiar sight when her father let her accompany him on medical calls, because British soldiers were stationed in New York City during most of the war.

At first she attended a small private school, but since educational opportunities for women were limited she later continued her education at home under her father's guidance. She made good use of his extensive library.

Her early notebooks indicate that she found religious and historical subjects particularly interesting. She enjoyed reading the scriptures, especially the Book of Psalms. A faithful Christian, baptized and confirmed in the Episcopal Church, she always wore a crucifix around her neck.

The social event of 1794 was the January wedding of Elizabeth Bayley and the wealthy young merchant, William Seton. Later, financially secure and happily married, Elizabeth continued as she had in the past to share her gifts with those who were not so fortunate. Her active concern for the poor and sick caused her to minister to them in such a way that she and her sister-in-law who accompanied her were called the "Protestant Sisters of Charity." In 1797, moved by the pain they saw in the city, these two women helped found a "Society for the Relief of Poor Widows with Small Children." At this time Elizabeth was the mother of two young children, Anna Marie and William.

In 1798, when Elizabeth was not quite 24, her husband's father died, and Elizabeth and her husband agreed to take his seven youngest children into their own home. Soon the Seton family business found itself in serious financial difficulties and Mr. Seton contracted tuberculosis. The doctor advised a long ocean voyage in the hope that a change in climate would improve his health. But this prescription was not easily carried out; by now Elizabeth and her husband had five children of their own. In addition to Anna Marie and William, Richard, Catherine and Rebecca were on the scene.

The Setons decided to take Anna Marie with them and to leave their four youngest children in the care of Mr. Seton's sister, Rebecca. The three Setons sailed for Leghorn, Italy, to visit old business friends, the Filicchi family. The trip on the *Shepherdess* took six weeks, and when they arrived in Italy, on November 19, 1803, they were quarantined for 30 days because of a rumor that there was a yellow fever epidemic in New York. They were made to stay in a cold, damp, almost bare, stone building, the Lazaretto, and during this detention Mr. Seton's health steadily declined. He died a short time after they were released.

Mrs. Seton and her daughter remained in Leghorn for about three months. The Filicchis took their guests on tours of art galleries and churches and did all they could to be of comfort during the time of their initial grief. This visit turned out to be a key to the rest of widow Seton's life.

The Filicchis were devout Catholics; praying together in the morning and evening was part of their everyday routine. Daily Mass was celebrated in the family chapel. With the Filicchis and in the Catholic churches of Italy Elizabeth became acquainted with and impressed by the Catholic religion.

When she returned to the United States, she faced a serious decision. Should she become a Catholic or remain an Episcopalian? In discussing the possible change she met vehement opposition from her family, friends and advisors, but strong encouragement from Catholic clergymen. She made her choice and was received into the Catholic faith on March 4, 1805, by Father Matthew O'Brien, pastor of St. Peter's Church, New York City. Many of her friends would have nothing more to do with her, and some of her relatives stopped helping her.

The next three years were very hard for the widow Seton as she struggled to support herself and her five children. Friends were very concerned about her financial problems. First, she opened a school for girls but it failed. Next she ran a boardinghouse for boys who were attending a successful private school. The Filicchi brothers provided funds for the education of her two boys, now seven and nine, and she thought seriously of taking her daughters with her to Canada to find some Catholic settlement where she could teach.

Then one autumn morning in 1806 she met Father (later Bishop) William DuBourg, a Sulpician priest who was president of St. Mary's College in Baltimore and who was visiting in New York. Their meeting was another turning point in Elizabeth Seton's life. DuBourg told her of his plan to open a school for Catholic girls in Baltimore. He mentioned that he was trying to find a qualified directress. It took a while to work out the details, but in June of 1808 Mrs. Seton moved to Baltimore with her children to open that Catholic girls' school. It was an immediate success.

In Baltimore, Elizabeth found a comfortable home and made many influential friends. Soon other women began to join her in her work. It was not long before she confided to Archbishop Carroll her desire to begin a religious community that would be devoted to teaching—a dream she had held since her visit with the Filicchi family five years before. She suggested that the sisters could dress in a contemporary way; she had already adopted the black dress and small bonnet of the Italian widow.

Archbishop Carroll suggested the rule of Saint Vincent de Paul, and on March 25, 1809, he named Elizabeth Seton "Mother." While waiting to decide officially on a rule of life, the group became known as the Saint Joseph Community. Shortly afterward a decision was made to open a school in Emmitsburg, Maryland.

In June, 1809, in a covered wagon, Mother Seton moved to Emmitsburg and began training teachers, preparing texts, translating religious books from French, visiting the poor and sick of the surrounding community. She opened the first American Catholic free school for girls, and it was followed within a few months by a school for boys. In January, 1812, 20 sisters voted to adopt the rule of the Sisters of Charity in France and in this way the American Congregation of the Sisters of Charity was formalized.

That same year her oldest daughter, Anna Marie, died at the age of 17. Rebecca, her youngest child, died four years later in 1816. Her two sons completed their education and began their careers with the Filicchi family in Italy. Her other daughter, Catherine, joined the Sisters of Mercy.

Mother Seton did not live a long time, but she knew the joys and sorrows of a full life. In 1814 she sent sisters to Philadelphia to open the first North American Catholic orphanage, and in 1817 another was opened in New York. In 1818 a free school was opened in Philadelphia and two years later another in New York. On January 4, 1821, Elizabeth Seton died at the age of 47. In 1959 she was declared Venerable. In 1963 she was beatified and on September 14, 1975, she became the first person born in America to be canonized.

The religious order which she started, the first religious society founded in this country, grew into one of the largest sisterhoods in the United States. Today there are six distinct families of the Sisters of Charity who work in North and South America, Italy and in the foreign missions.

In Washington, D. C., there is a statue of Elizabeth Seton at the

National Shrine of the Immaculate Conception and her portrait is part of the Saint-Memin collection at the Portrait Gallery.

Recommended Readings

Dirvin, Joseph I. *Mrs. Seton: Foundress of the Sisters of Charity.* New York: Farrar, Straus, Giroux, 1961.

Melville, Annabelle (McConnell). *Elizabeth Bayley Seton: Foundress of the American Sisters of Charity.* New York: Scribner's, 1960.

Learning Experience
Primary Level

TEACHER NOTES:

When you have shared with the children the major events of Elizabeth Seton's life, guide the class in a discussion of her experiences by questioning them in the following manner:

- What were some of the most difficult times in Elizabeth Seton's life?
- What did she do to try and overcome her problems?
- Was it easy to travel when Mother Seton lived?
- How did she share herself with others? How did she care for her family after Mr. Seton died? Why do you think she shared herself with people who were not part of her family?
- Were there any things that she did during her life that you thought were wrong?
- Have you ever known anyone who helped others as she did? Anyone in your own family?
- Why do you suppose Mother Seton's group of sisters took the name, Sisters of Charity?

LEARNING EXPERIENCE: Mural

When the children have had sufficient time to discuss the major events of her life, and have related them to their own experience, pass out shelf paper or mural paper and paint or magic markers and direct the children to create a mural depicting the events they felt were most memorable. When they have completed their drawings ask them to entitle their murals, "Our American Sister of Charity," and then hang the murals in the classroom. Using the artwork as a focal point, give the children an opportunity to add further comments they may have.

SUPPLIES:

Mural or shelf paper, paint, crayons or magic markers.

Learning Experience
Intermediate Level

TEACHER NOTES:

Once the class has heard Elizabeth Seton's story, involve them in a brief discussion of the kind of person she was. Lead them to support any kind of general statement ("She was generous") with at least one specific example from her life. Inquire whether she reminds them of anyone they've known or heard about and question them whether it makes any difference if we live our life for others or for ourselves.

LEARNING EXPERIENCE: Dramatization

Invite the youngsters to dramatize the story of Mother Seton's life either in the form of a narrated pantomime or a written dialogue. The following guide is not intended to limit the length of the play but rather to assist in its development. Your class may not need it at all. Use it if you think your youngsters would benefit from having a format to build around, and encourage them to improvise and create props and scenery for their production, too.

SUPPLIES:

Materials for making props and scenery.

Dramatization Guide

SCENE 1:

Location:
New York

Time:
1802

Characters:
Elizabeth and William Seton; their three daughters, Anna Marie, Catherine and Rebecca; their two sons, William and Richard; Aunt Rebecca, William Seton's sister; the family doctor.

Situation:
Mr. Seton, very upset by his business troubles, admits that he isn't feeling very well at all. Sympathetic and concerned, Mrs. Seton offers to do anything that will be of help. When the doctor

is consulted he admits that he doesn't know exactly what is wrong but thinks that a change in climate might be part of the cure. The family decides to visit their good friends, the Filicchi family, in Italy, and Aunt Rebecca invites the children to stay with her while their mother and father make this long voyage. Mrs. Seton agrees that the four youngest should stay but she suggests that Anna Marie could be a help to her in taking care of Mr. Seton.

SCENE 2:

Location:
Leghorn, Italy

Time:
November, 1803

Characters:
Elizabeth and William Seton; their daughter, Anna Marie; one or two immigration officer(s).

Situation:
It has taken the Seton family six weeks to cross the ocean on the ship *Shepherdess* and Mr. Seton's health is worse. When they land they are told that anyone traveling from New York will have to be quarantined for 30 days because of the news that there is an epidemic of yellow fever spreading through New York City. The three of them are directed to a cold, damp, almost bare stone building called the Lazaretto where they will be permitted to wait out the period of quarantine.

SCENE 3:

Location:
Leghorn, Italy, in the Filicchis' home

Time:
Six weeks later, January, 1804

Characters:
Elizabeth Seton, Anna Marie, Antonio Filicchi

Situation:
The Filicchi family invites Elizabeth Seton and her daughter, Anna Marie, to stay with them until they recover from the strain of the past weeks. Both families are saddened by the recent death of

Mr. Seton—Antonio Filicchi had been William Seton's best friend. The Setons enjoy a tour of the Filicchi home—seeing the family chapel where daily Mass is celebrated and learning that everybody comes together for prayers in the morning and evening and for the Rosary.

SCENE 4:

Location:
New York

Time:
March, 1805

Characters:
Elizabeth Seton, Rev. Matthew O'Brien

Situation:
The widow Seton talks with Father O'Brien about her desire to become a Catholic. She explains that this interest began when she saw how the lives of the Filicchi family members were affected by their beliefs. She is aware that her friends and relatives will not understand and will probably abandon her if she does change her religion. This saddens her, but more than anything she wants to be baptized in time for Easter. Elizabeth Seton is received into the Catholic faith in March in St. Peter's Church, New York.

NARRATOR:
The next three years were very hard for the widow Seton as she struggled to support herself and her five children. She opened a school but only a few students enrolled and it failed. She taught in a private school but was unhappy because of the prejudice that surrounded her and her family. In June, 1808, Mrs. Seton moved to Baltimore with her daughters to open a Catholic girls' school.

SCENE 5:

Location:
Paca Street, Baltimore

Time:
1808

Characters:
Five students; three women; Elizabeth Seton; Bishop Carroll

Situation:

Everybody is very busy. Girls are happily enrolling in widow Seton's school and young women are offering to assist the widow Seton in her work. Elizabeth confides to Bishop Carroll that she wants to begin a religious community that would dress simply and be devoted to teaching. Bishop Carroll thinks it over, suggests a set of rules and names Elizabeth Seton the first superior of the American Sisters of Charity by giving her the title of Mother.

NARRATOR:

In June, 1809, Mother Seton moved to Emmitsburg, Maryland, where she trained teachers, prepared textbooks, translated religious books from the French and visited the poor and sick of the neighborhood. In 1814 she sent sisters to Philadelphia to open the first Catholic orphanage and in 1817 one was opened in New York. She died in 1821. In 1959 she was declared Venerable, in 1963 she was beatified, and in 1975 she was canonized.

Learning Experience
Junior High Level

TEACHER NOTES:

After presenting the biography to the students, provide this setting for the class: The year is 1810. The place is your hometown, Emmitsburg, Maryland. You are writing a newsy letter to a favorite friend. Tell this person about your new neighbor, a widow, called Mother Seton.

LEARNING EXPERIENCE: Letter

Tell the students to include in their letters facts about her early life, her devotion to her husband and family, her husband's death, her change to Catholicism, and her struggle to support herself and her five children. Ask them to describe the way she dresses and the kinds of things you see her doing in the neighborhood. Have them include the reactions of some of your neighbors to the opening of the new "free" school and have them mention the rumors of the future establishment of orphanages and hospitals as well as your own ideas about "these American Sisters of Charity." Predict what people will be saying about Mother Seton in 150 to 200 years. When all have finished their letters, encourage them to share what they have written with the rest of the class.

SUPPLIES:

Paper, pencils.

John England (1786-1842)

"The dogmas of the quiet past are inadequate to the stormy present. The occasion is piled high with difficulty and we must rise with the occasion. As our case is new, so we must think anew, and act anew."
—Abraham Lincoln
Annual Message to Congress
(December 1862)

In August, 1790, Archbishop John Carroll was consecrated the first Catholic bishop of the United States. By 1808 the Church had begun to grow and the enormous American Mission was subdivided into six more manageable dioceses — Baltimore (Maryland), Bardstown (Kentucky), Boston (Massachusetts), New York (New York), Philadelphia (Pennsylvania), and the territory of Louisiana. Actually, Louisiana first became a diocese in 1793, when the territory was under Spanish control. In 1815, Carroll appointed Father William DuBourg Bishop of Louisiana and Florida, but since Louisiana was American and Florida was still Spanish at the time, unified ecclesiastical control was impossible.

When Carroll died on December 3, 1815, his coadjutor, a fellow Marylander, Leonard Neale, succeeded him. But Neale lived only 18 more months. The third Archbishop of Baltimore was the French Sulpician, Ambrose Marechal, who served the diocese for ten years from his consecration in 1818 until his death in 1828.

During the early part of Marechal's administration, Rome saw that the number of Catholics had increased from around 90,000 at the time of Carroll's death to 160,000 five years later, and in 1820 it created two

65

additional dioceses — one in Virginia with a see at Richmond, and another encompassing South Carolina, North Carolina and Georgia, with a see at Charleston. An enormously talented Irish priest with the remarkable name of John England was appointed bishop of the new Diocese of Charleston.

Born in County Cork and ordained at the age of 22, Father John England distinguished himself in Cork as a man of many talents and seemingly boundless energy. At one time he held 10 different positions simultaneously, including preacher, editor of a Catholic monthly, chaplain of the city prisons, professor of the diocesan seminary and diocesan superintendent of schools.

He was a reformer who worked to improve the conditions under which convicts were transported to Australia; through his newspaper campaign he aroused public opposition to the intolerable treatment of the Catholic prisoners in Australia. While he was chaplain to the Cork jail, his vigorous appeal to British Church and state authorities — in the form of an open letter dated January 5, 1819 — was responsible for the British government permitting non-Anglican clergymen in Australian penal settlements. As a direct result of these efforts, he is sometimes called the "founder of the Catholic Church in Australia" because freedom of conscience was allowed and a Catholic mission was established in Australia ten years before the Catholic Emancipation Act of 1829 was passed in England. In another disagreement with Britain this fiery Irish patriot, writing in the *Cork Mercantile Chronicle,* took an active part in the Veto Question and opposed the right of the British Crown to interfere in the selection of bishops in Ireland. Because of his activist support for "the underdog" in so many arenas, there are numerous suggestions that many were pleased when John England was appointed a bishop in the United States.

He and his sister Joanna and a friend, Father Denis Corkery, traveled on the ship *Thomas Getston* and arrived in Charleston on December 28, 1820. England immediately wrote Archbishop Marechal that he was beginning his work and issued a pastoral letter to the faithful, the first such letter in the history of the American Catholic Church. He had a particular interest in education so he prepared a missal and a catechism that could be used by all persons in his diocese. He also established a book society and a library. Having been an editor and a journalist in Ireland, Bishop John England was well acquainted with another instrument that could enlighten his own people and at the same time combat the charges being made against the Catholic Church. On June 5, 1822, he began the *United States Catholic Miscellany,* the first American Catholic weekly newspaper. This paper exerted strong influence on American Catholic thought and, during the next 20 years, other Catholic papers were established at the rate of one a year.

In 1825, dissatisfied with the French methods of training in the seminary at Baltimore, he decided to open his own diocesan seminary. He welcomed American as well as Irish seminarians. He found that he had to do much of the teaching himself and, though it took up a great deal of his time, he found that it also gave him the benefit of knowing the future priests of his diocese very well.

All kinds of difficulties arose when the members of the American Catholic Church insisted that the methods of American democracy extend even to Church matters. They sought a voice in matters that affected them. John England solved many complex problems but evoked Archbishop Marechal's disapproval when he drew up a diocesan constitution that established a house of laymen and a house of clergy. Both groups served in advisory capacities to Bishop England, much like diocesan councils today.

Bishop England constantly urged that a Provincial Council be held to discuss the problem of trusteeism* and to decide on standard regulations for the growing Catholic Church body in the United States. Archbishop Marechal never admitted the need for such a council, but when Marechal died, Bishop England wrote his successor, James Whitfield, and repeated his request that a Provincial Council be called. Other bishops, how many is not known, wrote to Whitfield urging the same and on December 18, 1828, Archbishop Whitfield announced that the First Provincial Synod would open on October 1, 1829.

Bishop England was well known as an orator and was even invited to address the United States Congress. On January 8, 1826, with President John Quincy Adams in attendance, the first Catholic clergyman to address Congress spoke for two hours on Catholicism. One month earlier he had received his final papers as a citizen of the United States.

Despite the general prejudice against Catholics and blacks, he started a school for free Negro children. In 1829, after visiting the newly formed Oblate Sisters of Providence in Baltimore who were operating the first school for black youngsters, he organized a diocesan community, the Sisters of Charity of Our Lady of Mercy, to help him teach the youngsters of his diocese. His concern that all people in his diocese have the opportunity to be educated angered the slaveholders and in 1835 he had to abandon the school.

His closest friend and advisor during the 22 years he served as Bishop of Charleston was a distinguished Catholic layman from North Carolina named William Gaston. Gaston had been the first student to enroll at Georgetown University and, for a while, its only student when it opened in 1791. Archbishop John Carroll advised Gaston to go on to Princeton where he graduated at the head of his class. He entered the law firm of Francis X. Martin and was admitted to the North Carolina bar at the age of 20. In 1800, he was elected to the North Carolina State Senate, served

---

*Refers to individuals who managed the money and property of a particular parish and could make decisions concerning them.

as a United States Senator during the War of 1812, and in 1825 he was awarded an honorary degree from Harvard. He held many posts, both elected and appointed, and from 1833 until his death in 1844 he served as an associate justice of the North Carolina Supreme Court. As a friend to the innovative John England, Gaston offered support during many dark days. He maintained a great interest in Bishop England's projects, especially his newspaper, and contributed both funds and articles.

John England was an outstanding person with many "firsts" to his credit. It is very likely that he heard the objection, "But, we've never done it *that* way!" whenever he suggested a creative approach to the social injustice he witnessed, the national prejudice he experienced, or the tensions between the hierarchy and the laity. His biographies indicate that he ran into strong opposition wherever he served, in Ireland and in the United States, and that his ideas were valued only after he had proven them successful himself.

When he arrived in South Carolina in 1820 there were close to 5,000 Catholics, a cathedral under construction in Charleston and three churches in Georgia. At the time of his death April 11, 1842, in Charleston, the diocese had 14 churches with three more under construction, 20 priests and a Catholic population of about 12,000.

Recommended Readings

> Greeley, Andrew M. *The Catholic Experience.* New York: Doubleday Image Books, 1967.
> Guilday, Peter. *The Life and Times of John England, First Bishop of Charleston (1786-1842).* New York: America Press, 1927.

Learning Experience
Primary Level

TEACHER NOTES:

As you relate the story of John England to the children stress the fact that, while Bishop of Charleston, he was seriously concerned about his Catholic population being educated, informed and permitted to worship freely in our country. Add that these great concerns influenced him to establish the first Catholic newspaper in America.

LEARNING EXPERIENCE: Guest Speaker

Provide an enriching learning experience for the children by arranging for a guest speaker from your diocesan newspaper to come into your class to comment on the value of a Catholic press. Interview the speaker beforehand and provide him or her with the information in your biographical sketch as well as certain points you might wish them to touch on, for example:

The Catholic press has a responsibility to inform the wider Catholic community of special events; to provide helpful information to the parents as primary religious educators; to report on various social, political and moral issues confronting the members of the Catholic community; and so on.

Encourage the children to articulate what they have learned about John England while their guest speaker is present and to ask questions as well. Make it a really special day by serving drinks and snacks for the children and guest speaker to enjoy together after their dialogue.

SUPPLIES:
Drinks and snacks.

Learning Experience
Intermediate Level

TEACHER NOTES:
When the youngsters have had time to digest the data in the biography about John England, invite them to become a news-gathering agency.

LEARNING EXPERIENCE: Commemorative Newspaper Edition
Tell the youngsters that they are to write and compile articles (poetry, editorials) on the life and times of John England for a special commemorative issue of the (fictitious) *Today's Catholic Miscellany*. Ask them to draw maps and pictures to appear in their edition and to highlight through their stories the major events and issues concerning John England and the Catholic religious community between 1822, the first year England published his newspaper, and 1842, the year of his death. Instruct the youngsters to assemble their work on newsprint from their own diocesan newspaper as a background for the materials they have developed and put their creation on display for everyone in the class to view and review.

SUPPLIES:
Newsprint from any old copies of your diocesan newspaper, pencils, pens, magic markers, crayons, paste or tape, scissors, construction paper.

Learning Experience
Junior High Level

TEACHER NOTES:
After having related the data in the biographical sketch to the students, bring them to a greater awareness of the valuable contributions of John England and our American Catholic heritage by involving them in the creation of a "news broadcast." The news broadcast should provide

a broad overview of the character and accomplishments of John England, and it should be heard "on the air" a few hours before he gave his unprecedented speech to Congress on January 8, 1826.

LEARNING EXPERIENCE: News Broadcast

Challenge the students to use a modern format and draw from their own observations of everyday media coverage of important events. Encourage them to use an anchorman, on-the-spot reporters and personal interviews with England's advisors, friends, students, laypeople in his diocese and even prominent political personages. Although much of the content will be fictionalized, ask the students to gather pertinent data for their scenario from the information provided in the biography and if possible you should allow time and space to dramatize their production.

SUPPLIES:

Simple props and costumes, although not necessary, would enhance the learning experience.

Elizabeth Lange (1783-1882)

"I have a dream that one day men will rise up and come to see that they are made to live as brothers . . . that one day every Negro in this country, every colored person in the world, will be judged on the basis of the content of his character rather than the color of his skin."

— Martin Luther King, Jr.

There has never been a biography written about Elizabeth Lange, or a statue dedicated to her memory. But the few threads of documented information about her life, plus the oral tradition of the religious order she began, can be woven together to create a brilliant tapestry of a great American Catholic. Since her contributions to our Catholic American heritage were shaped by her experience as a woman of Negro ancestry, it is important to focus on the circumstances surrounding her life in the late 18th century to gain a clear perspective of her greatness.

When Elizabeth Lange was born in 1783, the Caribbean Islands were in a state of political chaos. Haiti, which was controlled by the economically powerful French, had a population made up of white Europeans (French and Spanish), black native Haitians, forcibly imported African Negro slaves, and mulattos who were the product of black and white intermarriages. Unfortunately, anyone who was not of "white only" origin, was designated by the white ruling class as "colored" and both the well-to-do and the impoverished in this category suffered the tragedies of oppression.

Haiti and the neighboring islands of Jamaica and San Domingo, which were occupied by the French and Spanish colonial governments, were the scene of many protests by black people. Frequently, the protests grew into uprisings against the harsh treatment by white landowners, and bloody massacres ensued. Before her birth, Elizabeth Lange's family fled from Haiti to Jamaica and then on to Cuba in an effort to avoid these conflicts.

Little is known about her father but it is certain that her mother, Annette Lange, gave birth to Elizabeth in the city of Santiago, Cuba, in

73

the province of Oriente which had become a haven for many black people escaping the racial antagonisms of the islands. There she was brought up in the Catholic faith and was educated in French, her family's native tongue, and Spanish, the language of Cuba. In the early part of the 19th century, in hopes that they could spare Elizabeth once again from the political turmoil of the islands, her parents secured passage for her, with the help of a friendly sea captain, on a sailing ship bound for the port of Charleston.

After arriving safely in Charleston, she is thought to have made her way to Norfolk, and then on to Baltimore, Maryland, by seeking the aid of sympathetic friends along the way and by "passing" as white because of her fair skin. There is some evidence that her white grandfather, Mardoche Lange, had emigrated to Baltimore at about the same time and, though he could not associate with her publicly because of their difference in "color," he may have arranged for her to purchase a modest residence in the city.

In Baltimore she had found physical refuge among other French- and Spanish-speaking islanders who had fled before her, but her painful journey had made it quite clear that the slavery mentality in America would offer no real refuge from racial discrimination. Elizabeth Lange realized that her people would have to bear many abuses in this country, but she saw as most devastating its laws denying black children an education. She knew that illiteracy would relegate black people to a status of inferiority as binding as the chains of slavery many of them had known in their island homes and would prevent them from learning more about their faith as well.

Confident that her own education and deep faith would be a source of enrichment and hope for the illiterate black children in her community, Elizabeth Lange used some money provided by her parents upon her departure from Cuba to set up a small free school in her home. Although her first students were children of other black refugees from the Caribbean Islands who spoke only French or Spanish, in time it grew to include many other poor black children from the area. The curriculum she followed was very simple: reading, writing, needlework and some time spent every day reading scripture with the children.

Not long after she had begun her school, she met another black refugee from the Caribbean Islands, Elizabeth Balas, who shared her love for children and her deep concern for their welfare. They also shared a deep faith and soon became good friends. Elizabeth Lange encouraged her friend to teach in the small school and the two worked closely together dedicating themselves to the education of poor black children for the next 10 years.

At about the time Miss Lange had sought refuge in America, members of the French clergy had begun to emigrate here to escape political upheaval caused by the revolution in their homeland. One of these priests, Father James Joubert, a member of the French Sulpician order, was instructed by his superiors to minister to the French-speaking Catholics of St. Mary's Church next to the Sulpician Seminary. "People of color," although they were never permitted to worship in the main section of the church, were a part of Father Joubert's parish too. In 1827, in the basement chapel where the services for the "colored" French-speaking Catholics were held, after Mass, he took charge of his first catechism class. Much to his dismay, he was confronted with a classroom of children who could not read or write. Unable to give them any formal religious instruction because of their illiteracy, Father Joubert dismissed them. He was appalled by the youngsters' desperate need for an education.

Since he was unaware of Elizabeth Lange's school, Father Joubert came up with what he thought was an original idea—to establish a school nearby for black children. He proposed the idea to Archbishop Whitfield of the diocese and convinced him that his plan to educate Negro girls would benefit "the society at large." Archbishop Whitfield consented to support the project and told Father Joubert to work out the details.

Within the next few weeks, probably in the basement chapel of St. Mary's, Father Joubert came to know Elizabeth Lange and her dear friend, Elizabeth Balas. When he visited Miss Lange's home he saw of course that she had been hard at work educating the very youngsters for whom he had been so concerned. Impressed by her compassion, dedication and deeply spiritual nature, Father Joubert suggested that she consider forming a religious society around which a more permanent school for Negro children could be maintained and even expanded.

Elizabeth Lange was overjoyed by Father Joubert's suggestion and immediately revealed to him that the formation of a religious order was a dream she and Elizabeth Balas had had for years. Because there were no religious orders open to black women at the time, regardless of their noble personal qualities, their dream until this moment had seemed utterly beyond fulfillment. The next day, Miss Lange told another San Domingan refugee, Rosina Boegue, who had been volunteering her services as a teacher at the school, about Father Joubert's idea and she too wanted to be a part of the new order.

Elizabeth Lange's personal funds were exhausted, so Father Joubert and two friends, Mrs. Chartard and Mrs. Ducatel, who were prominent white women in Baltimore, assisted the "three" candidates in setting up quarters where their religious family could live and operate their school. On June 13, 1828, a house was rented, and the "sisters" began their novitiate. The pupils in Miss Lange's school, which had expanded to 11 boarders and nine day students, moved in with them along with several orphans and a young Baltimorean, Almaide Duchemin, who had been a boarder but now expressed a desire to be a part of their religious community.

The general attitude of white people in the city—that women "of color" were not worthy of wearing a religious habit—created many difficulties for the "sisters" from the start. Elizabeth Lange, nevertheless, as their temporary superior, encouraged them to wear the distinctive garb they had selected to signify their community and to continue with their ministry in spite of the blatant prejudice around them.

Finally on July 2, 1829, Father Joubert blessed and heard the promises of Sister Mary (Lange), Sister Mary Frances (Balas), Sister Rose (Boegue), and Sister Theresa (Duchemin), and the formal reception of the very first religious order for Negro women in the history of the Church took place. As servants of God and his people they chose to wear a black dress, cape and white bonnet similar to that worn by the French peasantry and they called themselves Oblates (from the Latin for a person dedicated to some work), Sisters of Providence. The Rule they adopted firmly stated that they "consecrate themselves to God in a special manner not only to sanctify themselves and thereby secure the greater Glory of God, but also to work for the Christian education of colored children." It was faithfully and explicitly followed when in September they opened the first school for Negro children taught by Negro sisters in the United States.

Guided by its foundress and first officially elected superior, Sister Mary, the religious community prospered and in October, 1829, their school was visited by many bishops, including John England of Charleston who observed their organization and teaching methods in hopes of beginning a similar school in his own diocese. In 1832, Archbishop Stirling of Baltimore called on the Oblates to nurse the poor in the city's almshouse hospital when a cholera epidemic hit Baltimore. Led by Sister Mary, many of them tirelessly cared for the sick until the disease subsided.

With the death of their spiritual advisor, friend and champion, Father Joubert, in 1843, the order began to decline. The Sulpicians withdrew their support entirely because of teaching commitments of the order, and Archbishop Eccleston who had charge of the diocese offered them no assistance. By 1845, they had no chaplain and they had to travel through the streets to attend Mass, often being ridiculed along the way. Although they managed to keep their school in operation, they had to take in ironing and mending to keep themselves and the orphans they cared for from starving. With the order seemingly doomed to extinction, many members returned to their homes or chose to serve elsewhere.

The fear that all hope for the black apostolate would be lost if the order failed haunted Sister Mary. She took a job with a steady salary as a domestic worker at the Sulpician Seminary in Baltimore. A copy of a letter Sister Mary wrote to the rector of the seminary is on file in the Oblates Archives in Baltimore shows her a pioneer for women's rights. It clearly outlines the terms of employment she and the other sisters would accept, the duties they would assume and the working conditions they thought adequate.

Help came to the community in 1847 through the influence of Father

Neuman, then provincial for the Redemptorist Fathers stationed in Baltimore. He arranged for a retreat to be given to the remaining sisters, urging them to continue their ministry and assigned a German-born priest, Father Thaddeus Anwander, to assist them. When Father Anwander saw their "very bad state of abandonment," as he later wrote, he quickly became a new champion for their cause, literally begging on his knees before the Archbishop to lend his support so that the Oblates might be saved.

Sister Mary died in 1882, with Father Anwander at her bedside, but the work she pioneered is carried on today in schools, diocesan supervisory positions, federal programs, day-care centers, and intercommunity projects by over 200 Oblate Sisters of Providence. A prayer book, a cane and an inkwell belonging to her are displayed in a glass case at the Oblates Motherhouse in Baltimore, and they remind us of her piety, perseverance and her commitment to the education of black children. Although relics of the past, they can inspire each of us as Catholic Americans to continue her work in the future.

Recommended Readings

Reasons, George and Patrick, Sam. *They Had a Dream, Volume III.* Los Angeles: Los Angeles Times Syndicate, 1971.

Sherwood, Grace. *The Oblates' Hundred and One Years.* New York: Macmillan and Co., 1931.

Learning Experience
Primary Level

TEACHER NOTES:

After you have related the biography of Elizabeth Lange to the children, briefly review the milestones in her life by challenging them to recall the important people she knew and worked with. As the children identify the characters who were part of the story, either by name or description, print the names of each character on a separate index card or piece of construction paper (approximately 8" x 5"). Use the following list to call to their attention any important people they may have missed and take a few moments to discuss with them how each character related to Elizabeth Lange. Important characters in the life story of Elizabeth Lange: Annette Lange (Elizabeth Lange's mother), Friendly Sea Captain, Elizabeth Balas, Rosina Boegue, Almaide Duchemin, Father James Joubert, Bishop Whitfield, Mrs. Chartard, Mrs. Ducatel, Bishop John England, Bishop Eccleston, Father Anwander, the black students Elizabeth Lange taught.

LEARNING EXPERIENCE: Dramatization Game

Shuffle the cards on which you have written the names of the characters in Elizabeth Lange's story and involve them in a dramatization game.

Permit each child to select from the pile the name of a character to dramatize and have the other children take turns "playing" Elizabeth Lange.
Help the youngsters along by setting the scene for the situation they should
"act out" with their characters and encourage them to be creative with
their "reenactment." Provide "dress-ups" if possible for the children to wear
during their performances, and emphasize that they should portray each
situation as they "imagine" it might have happened.

SUPPLIES:
Index cards, "dress-ups."

Learning Experience
Intermediate Level

TEACHER NOTES:
Review the story of Elizabeth Lange's life with the youngsters after
you have shared the biography with them by challenging them to recall the
major events of her life in chronological order. Appoint someone in the
class to jot down important happenings on separate pieces of paper as they
are brought up and when they have finished, "fill in" any significant parts
they have missed. The following is not intended to limit the review but
rather to provide a sketchy outline for you to use as a ready reference in
guiding and stimulating their recollection of Elizabeth Lange's life:

1. Trip to America.
2. Journey from Charleston to Baltimore.
3. Conditions in Baltimore.
4. Elizabeth Lange's first free school for black children.
5. Father Joubert's experiences with the catechism class.
6. Meeting between Father Joubert and Elizabeth Lange.
7. Novitiate and formal reception of the "sisters" as Oblates.
8. Visit by Bishop England.
9. Helping in the cholera epidemic.
10. Death of Father Joubert and beginning of "hard times."
11. Father Anwander's assistance.
12. The Oblates today.

LEARNING EXPERIENCE: Audiovisual "Documentary"
Using the youngsters' review of the significant events in Elizabeth
Lange's life as a basis, challenge the youngsters to produce an audiovisual
"documentary" about her. Take a few moments to instruct the youngsters
in the techniques of working with the particular type of medium you have
selected for them, distribute the materials and then separate them into groups
of three.

Assign each group several situations, happenings or events in her life, and make it responsible for creating a series of visual frames depicting those events. Then choose one person from each group to prepare the audio-narration of their group's section of the documentary. When each group has completed its "assignment," organize the frames done in each group in chronological order and synchronize the audio-script (or tape recording) the students have prepared with the complete frames. After previewing the work with the class, invite guests to be enriched and entertained by the documentary the youngsters have produced about this Great American Catholic!

SUPPLIES:
Materials for creating "visual" presentation, several tape recorders. [Many different types of materials for creating visual presentations as described in the learning experience are available and can be easily handled by intermediate level youngsters. To name a few: transparencies (for use with overhead projector), U-Film, blank slides (for use with slide projector), exposed film (for use with filmstrip projector), freehand drawings on ordinary paper (for use with opaque projector).]

Learning Experience
Junior High Level

TEACHER NOTES:
Give the students time to explore and reflect on the biography of Elizabeth Lange and then focus their attention specifically on the difficulties she must have encountered in establishing her order and school for black children. Stimulate discussion by asking:
* What was the attitude of the white community in Baltimore, Maryland (a slaveholding state), toward blacks in 1829?
* Where and how do you suppose Elizabeth Lange would contact youngsters to attend her school?
* What problems might arise in finding facilities for her community to live and work in?
* How might she obtain funds for the operation of the community and school?

LEARNING EXPERIENCE: One-Minute Speech and Research Project
Remind the students that originally Father Joubert and two white women from the community, Mrs. Chartard and Mrs. Ducatel, helped Elizabeth Lange set up the school and community, and then tell them to imagine that they are one of the "three," in Baltimore, in 1829.
Tell them to prepare a one-minute speech to be given at a dinner to raise funds and support for the Oblates and their school. Since they are

seeking widespread support for the Oblates, tell the students that actually speeches must be given at three separate dinners in the city for three different segments of the population: one dinner for Catholic religious (bishops, priests and nuns); one dinner for prominent white people, and one dinner for the black community. Caution the students that they must keep in mind the attitudes of the audience they will be speaking to and encourage them to be as convincing as possible, including substantial reasons why the religious community and school should be supported. Arbitrarily assign each student to one of the three fund-raising dinners, give them sufficient time to prepare their speeches and then have them deliver them. Invite the class to ask questions of the "speaker" and comment on the speech as if they actually represented each of the three segments of the population.

The students may wish to broaden their learning experience by researching information about the black apostolate in their diocese. They may write to their Diocesan Chancery Office to obtain data on the number of blacks in their diocese and just how the diocese is meeting the needs of black Catholics in their area. They may also wish to write to the National Office of Black Catholics, Washington, D.C., for more information.

Paraliturgical Celebration for Unit II
Shaping a Nation

Theme:

Elizabeth Seton, John Carroll, John England and Elizabeth Lange have gone before us to share faith and hope and love with their fellow Americans. May we rejoice today in their courage and dedication, and celebrate the good news of their faith and work.

Entrance Hymn:

"Enter, Rejoice and Come In," Ray Repp, *Come Alive,* F.E.L.; "Till All My People Are One," Ray Repp, *Come Alive,* F.E.L.; "Maryland, My Maryland," James Randall, *The Story of Our National Ballads,* Thomas Y. Crowell Co.

Penitential Rite:

For the times you have called us to free others in need but we have not responded with charity, Lord, have mercy.

LORD, HAVE MERCY.

For the times you have called us to insist on fair treatment for all our brothers and sisters, but we have not had the courage, Christ have mercy.

CHRIST, HAVE MERCY.

For your patient love and understanding when we fail to listen for your call, Lord, have mercy.

LORD, HAVE MERCY.

First Reading:

(Isaiah 50:4-7) or "Prayer for the Civil Authorities," written by John Carroll, 1791:

We pray Thee, O God of might, wisdom and justice! through whom authority is rightly administered, laws are enacted, and judgment decreed, assist with Thy holy spirit of counsel and fortitude the President of the United States, that his administration may be conducted in righteousness, and be eminently useful to Thy people over

81

whom he presides; by encouraging due respect for virtue and religion; by a faithful execution of the laws of justice and mercy; and by restraining vice and immorality. Let the light of Thy divine wisdom direct the deliberations of Congress, and shine forth in all the proceedings and laws framed for our rule and government, so that they may tend to the preservation of peace, the promotion of national happiness, the increase of industry, sobriety and useful knowledge; and may perpetuate to us the blessing of equal liberty.

Gospel Reading:
(Luke 6:27-35)

Homily:
Bring the children to the realization that the people they have come to know through their learning experiences are admired because of the way they put their beliefs into action—their lives were rich in love and service to others.

Song:
"All That We Have," Gary Ault, *Tell the World*, F.E.L.; "Of My Hands," Ray Repp, *Hymnal for Young Christians*, F.E.L.; "Day by Day," Stephen Schwartz, *Godspell*, Celebration Services, Ltd.; "They'll Know We Are Christians," Peter Scholtes, *Worship*, G.I.A.; "We Shall Overcome," traditional.

Meditation:
Play a recording of "The Prayer of St. Francis" or "We've Been to the Mountain" in the background and, using either an opaque projector or an overhead projector with transparencies, present a visual collage of words and pictures which remind the youngsters of important events in the lives of the Catholic Americans they have meaningfully explored through the learning experiences in this unit. If possible have several of the youngsters work together in preparing the collage beforehand.

Recessional:
"Men of Faith, Women of Faith," Carey Landry, *Songs of Praise and Reconciliation*, N.A.L.R.; "God Bless America," Irving Berlin, *The Story of Our National Ballads*, Thomas Y. Crowell Co.; "Mine Eyes Have Seen the Glory," *Worship*, G.I.A.

NOTE: Use as much of the work developed in the original learning experiences as possible. In the entrance procession some youngsters may carry artwork.

UNIT III

Era of Expansion and Industrialization

Pierre-Jean DeSmet (1801-1873)

"It is my nature to rejoice with those who rejoice and weep with those who weep. . . ."
— Pierre-Jean DeSmet

When Pierre-Jean DeSmet left his home in the Belgian village of Termonde for the untamed wilderness of the American frontier, it was with mixed emotions. His family and friends thought this decision was an outrageous sacrifice and vehemently disapproved of his leaving. He was an intelligent, athletic and handsome young man who had distinguished himself at the seminary of Malines and his family had hoped he would pursue a profession in law or diplomacy.

In his last year at school his parents were still unaware of his deep convictions, even though he showed enthusiasm for the faith and the study of Church history. It was not until he met Father Charles Nerinckx, a Jesuit priest visiting Belgium in search of applicants for the Jesuit Order in the United States, that his parents finally realized his intentions. Pierre DeSmet was inspired by Nerinckx's vivid descriptions of the unchartered lands and the native Americans among whom the Jesuits would sow the seeds of Christianity. Convinced of the urgency of Father Nerinckx's request and his own personal call to service, Pierre decided to share his faith as a Jesuit missionary among the Indians of the American frontier. In the summer of 1821, he and five other homesick and scared young men made the 40-day voyage across the Atlantic with Father Nerinckx.

When their ship docked in Philadelphia, their first glimpse of the city bore no resemblance to the wilderness Father Nerinckx had described. The novices were astonished to see well-constructed buildings and well-dressed inhabitants in the city. The scene soon changed, however, as they met their master of Jesuit novices in the United States, Father Charles Van Quickenbourne, and traveled to the rather dilapidated residence in

White Marsh, Maryland, where they would continue their studies for the priesthood.

While the young novices spent the next 18 months in relative seclusion at White Marsh, the expansion which had characterized American life since Lewis and Clark's exploration of the vast Louisiana Territory in 1804 intensified. The white population was pushing through the Appalachian Mountains at an ever-increasing speed and the unfortunate result was the complete and absolute disruption of the land which had been the exclusive domain of the American Indian.

White people on all social, economic and educational levels generally held the attitude that the Indian was a heathen, a primitive, a "lesser" race and an annoying obstacle to the extension of civilization. When the Indian would not relinquish his land to the white man, he was considered a potential threat that had to be either removed or annihilated. The land, so prized by both the white man and the Indian, was the issue and the point of bloody confrontation. On one side stood the white man with the burning aspiration and technology to buy, sell, till, graze, mine and exploit the land. On the other side stood the Indian who cherished its power to feed, strengthen, cleanse, to heal and comfort its people as an "Earth Mother," to be equally claimed by all but sacredly revered and never conquered.

The Shawnee Chief Tecumseh, who attempted in vain to rally the Indian nations east of the Mississippi in order to preserve their hold on the land, expressed the Indian attitude toward the white man's concept of "real estate," "Sell a country! Why not sell the air, the great sea, as well as the earth?"

The administration of James Monroe had already accepted a "removal policy" toward the Indian when Pierre-Jean DeSmet set foot on this bitterly contested soil. The Indians were given no choice; they were told emphatically that they must yield to the surge of white expansion and move to designated areas west of the Mississippi. It was due to this policy that the Jesuits at White Marsh were drawn to St. Louis, Missouri, to establish a school and mission for Indian boys. Since the order already owned property in the St. Louis area, Bishop Dubourg of Louisiana encouraged the move and the then Secretary of War, John Calhoun, informed the Society that the government would guarantee a subsidy of $800 per year for their missionary endeavors.

Packing all the tools, books and treasured religious articles they could manage in three wagons, the group journeyed for five weeks by foot, flatboat and steamboat to St. Louis. With their arrival in the ramshackle frontier town, the hardships of the trip were soon forgotten and Pierre DeSmet's enthusiasm for beginning his new apostolate soared. Fifteen miles north of St. Louis, on farmland near the Missouri River, and adjacent to the village of Florissant, a site was selected for the first log structure to house the novitiate.

Although only 5'7" tall, Pierre DeSmet's muscular body was a power-ful asset to the small community as they labored to complete their first building. The nickname of "Samson" given Pierre DeSmet in his home-town in Belgium appropriately described his physical prowess and his strong determination to achieve his spiritual goals as well. Once log cabins for the schoolrooms and mission were completed, he worked inexhaustibly with his Indian students.

After one year, however, the combined efforts of the entire community to "civilize" the Indians were to no avail. The Indians who had been ac-customed to a transient, nomadic life-style were not obliged to take on the responsibilities of mission life which included cooking and farming as well as studying, and the project ended in failure. Father Van Quickenbourne decided to keep the mission and novitiate open on a small scale but to abandon the present school and focus attention on the educational needs of the swiftly growing white population in the immediately surrounding area.

Pierre DeSmet and his fellow novices were ordained in 1827 and Bishop Dubourg, who had established St. Louis College nine years ear-lier, quickly made a request that the Jesuits put their talents to work as faculty members there. The news of his appointment to the college staff was a deep disappointment to Father DeSmet. He longed for a deeper understanding of the Indian culture and another opportunity to share his own with them. Nevertheless, he accepted his teaching duties and took on the added job of supervising and procuring supplies for the building of new churches, schools and convents in booming St. Louis.

In 1831, the Provincial Council in Baltimore proposed and Rome approved the plan that all the Indian missions in the United States be placed under the jurisdiction of the Jesuits. With the immense territory to the west open to missionary work, the possibility of being given an Indian assignment excited Father DeSmet once again. Unfortunately, he was suddenly stricken with a strange illness which sapped his strength and it became necessary for him to take leave of absence and recuperate in Belgium. Before he left in 1833, he became a United States citizen, dramatically underscoring his sincere intentions to return to America and the Indian apostolate.

It wasn't until 1837 that Father DeSmet, his health fully restored, came back to America. While abroad, he had involved himself whenever possible in the recruitment of men and the procurement of valuable equipment for the St. Louis University and the Missouri Novitiate of the Society of Jesus. A very grateful faculty welcomed the robust and good-humored Father DeSmet upon his return, and his superiors happily told him of their plans for his next assignment — to found a mission among the Potawatomi Indians! Father DeSmet was overjoyed with the news and eagerly set out to accomplish the work which was closest to his heart.

On his way up the Missouri River to the Potawatomi tribe (located in the present vicinity of Council Bluffs, Iowa), Father DeSmet stopped often to visit with many other tribes. This practice and the fastidious writing of a journal to record the events of each day, the language, dress, customs and religious beliefs of the Indians he encountered, as well as his observations of the terrain and wildlife, were to set a precedent which he was to follow throughout his distinctive career. He also wrote long letters regularly communicating similar information to friends in the United States and Europe in the hope of bringing the outside world to a deeper understanding and appreciation of the many different tribes, cultures and beliefs.

The Potawatomi mission, called St. Joseph's, was established and Father DeSmet was then commissioned to survey the possibilities for Catholic missions in the Oregon country. From that time, the scope of his activities widened to include missionary work in the Pacific Northwest as well as the Great Plains. He continually sought recruits, equipment and moral support for his missions by propagandizing the Indian cause in the large Eastern cities, in New Orleans, and throughout Europe in Ireland, England, Holland, Belgium, France and Italy. In carrying out his projects he is known to have crossed the Atlantic Ocean 16 times and traveled over 180,000 miles.

In September of 1841, Father DeSmet founded the St. Mary's mission among the Flathead Tribe in northwestern Montana, the Mission of St. Ignatius among the Kalispels and the Sacred Heart Mission among the Coeur d' Alenes in northern Idaho. Before 1846, nearly all the native populations of the Columbia Valley had also been touched by his warm and friendly personality. "Blackrobe," as he was called east of the Rockies, was held in high esteem by the Sioux and the Blackfeet and many other tribes east of the Rockies as well.

Father DeSmet often lamented in his writings to Church officials and to friends that there were too few priests to preach the Good News

about the "Great Spirit" to the Indians. Many of his letters and journals testify to incidents when various Indian chiefs and tribesmen begged him to establish missions and schools in their territories because they were convinced that his efforts were dedicated to their welfare. For the most part, his requests for more priests to minister to the Indians were denied because of other priorities. Many great opportunities to help the Indians were lost.

Father DeSmet did everything in his power to improve the physical and spiritual condition of the Indians. Besides administering the sacraments and preaching whenever they were receptive, he became a self-styled physician when they were afflicted with disease and an emissary of peace when trouble arose between rival tribes. In their interest he waged a vigorous campaign against the Federal Government (specifically Indian Department officials) for permitting the devastating flood of liquor to the Indians. Unfortunately, the indictments he penned against the liquor traffic went unheeded and the problem continued to plague the Indians throughout Father DeSmet's lifetime.

By 1850, the mass exodus of fortune seekers moving westward through the Indian territory had left many natives destitute and homeless. The Indians fought the encroachment of their land with force and Father DeSmet was often asked by the government to quell uprisings and act as mediator for the negotiation of treaties. Aware that the best interests of the Indians were generally not considered when the treaties were drawn up and that the terms of the treaties would probably be violated by white men even before the ink on the document had dried, he nevertheless participated because he saw negotiation as the only way to avert violence and gain the Indian some measure of improvement.

His most notable achievement in Indian diplomacy was in June, 1868, when in an attempt to achieve a lasting peace, he entered the camp of Sitting Bull in the Valley of the Bighorn in present-day South Dakota. Although the braves had sworn to take the life of the first white man to show himself among them, at the sight of his "Black Robe," the Sioux warriors rode forward to shake his hand.

When Father DeSmet noted in his journal, "It is my nature to rejoice with those who rejoice and weep with those who weep . . .," he revealed a valuable clue to his successful achievements in the missionary field and his greatness as a Catholic American. It was by sharing in the daily experiences of the American Indian and forever seeking to understand and appreciate their culture and faith that Pierre-Jean DeSmet meaningfully shared his own faith with them.

Recommended Readings

Horn, Huston and the Editors of Time-Life Books. *The Pioneers.* New York: Time-Life Books, 1974. (Pages 68-72.)

Terrell, John Upton. *Blackrobe: The Life of Pierre-Jean DeSmet, Missionary, Explorer and Pioneer.* New York: Doubleday, 1964.

Learning Experience
Primary Level

TEACHER NOTES:

After telling the children the story of Peter DeSmet, talk to them about the feelings both the Indians and Father DeSmet must have had when they first met. Remind the children that the Indian and the white man spoke different languages, dressed differently and even ate different foods. Use pictures from magazines, encyclopedias and books which pertain to the Indians of the American plains and the Northwest to enrich the discussion and ask them to think about ways in which they could "talk" to one another without using words, either spoken or written down. Guide the children in a discussion of the various art forms the Indians use to communicate their thoughts and to tell the story of their people. Focus the children's attention specifically on the Indian totem pole often constructed by a tribe to relate the story of their past.

LEARNING EXPERIENCE: Construct a Totem Pole

Separate the children into groups of three or four, provide them with cardboard boxes of varying sizes, masking tape and magic markers, and invite them to create a sculpture similar to the totem poles constructed by the Indians in America in the 19th century. Tell them to imagine that they all are members of an Indian tribe in the Northwest who have had Father DeSmet as a guest in their village for several weeks and ask them to tell about the things he said and did by drawing pictures and symbols on their "totem poles."

SUPPLIES:

Cardboard boxes, magic markers, masking tape (staples and brads may also be used to join the boxes to create the totem pole sculpture).

Learning Experience
Intermediate Level

TEACHER NOTES:

Relate the story of Peter DeSmet to the youngsters, and when they have had sufficient time to reflect on what they have heard, ask them to explain what they think he meant when he wrote in his journal, "It is my nature to rejoice with those who rejoice and weep with those who weep. . . ."

Guide them in a discussion of the kinds of activities they think may have been part of Father DeSmet's day while he visited an Indian village or camp. Include the things he and the Indians may have talked about together, enjoyed together, and even suffered together. Have the students jot down on paper as many differences in culture and beliefs as they can think of. Concentrate on features the Indians and Father DeSmet normally would not have had in common — but which they could have shared when he visited them.

LEARNING EXPERIENCE: Mobile

Point out to the youngsters that even though there were many differences between Father DeSmet's and the Indians' culture, customs and beliefs, there were also a great many experiences, ideas and hopes that they had in common.

Give the youngsters hangers or wooden dowels, yarn or cord, scissors, magic markers and colored construction paper. Ask them to make a mobile using symbols, words and pictures of the many things Father DeSmet and the Indians shared and which helped their respect, trust and love for one another grow.

SUPPLIES:

Construction paper, scissors, yarn or cord, wire hangers or wooden dowels, magic markers.

Learning Experience
Junior High Level

TEACHER NOTES:

When the students have fully explored the biography of Peter DeSmet, ask them to reflect on his life and try to recall the many problems and obstacles he and the Indian tribes encountered in the years following their first experience together in Florissant, Missouri. Encourage the youngsters to explain both the problems they identify and the results. Appoint someone to record their contributions on the chalkboard.

LEARNING EXPERIENCE: Story

Ask the students to look back in history and try to imagine what it would be like if things had been different. Tell them to stretch their imaginations and think about what it would be like today if circumstances, people, or events had not presented obstacles in the paths of the Indians or of Father DeSmet. Then ask them to write a short story or paragraph containing their ideas. When they finish invite them to share what they have written and make a corresponding list of all the people who could have helped the Indians to preserve their civilization rather than destroy it. Help the students to understand that there were many people then as there are today who could have "made a difference" in the Indians' lives, possibly even changed the course of history, had they attempted to understand the Indians' customs, culture, beliefs and religious heritage.

SUPPLIES:

Paper, pencils.

Orestes Brownson (1803-1876)*

". . . Conversion is the work of grace, not of argument or logic."
— Orestes Brownson

When a mother has young children, usually most of her time is spent in caring for the needs and development of the family. The same can be said of the Catholic Church in the United States during the 19th century. She was busy establishing a unique American home and trying to tend to the needs of her new immigrant arrivals. The Church recognized that much had to be done in the matters of education, culturalization and spiritual development, and she slowly became aware of the social and moral problems which were mounting as the population grew. On the scene appeared Orestes Brownson, a Catholic convert, an active reformer, a self-educated, restless man who jolted America with his eloquent outcries against social injustice.

Orestes Brownson was born, with a twin sister, Daphne, on September 16, 1803, on a small farm in Stockbridge, Vermont. When Brownson's father died two years later, his mother found she could not manage the support of her six children. When Orestes was six, he was sent to live with an elderly couple in Royalton, Vermont.

Books on the theology of the Congregational faith were his companions. He was taken to worship services occasionally and was raised to be moral, honest, truthful and righteous. By his 12th birthday, he could no longer accept the religion of his foster parents and, after much thought, studied Methodism.

Two years later he was reunited with his mother and the rest of his family in Ballston Spa, New York, and briefly attended a neighboring school. This was the only formal education he received.

During the next three decades he wrote for a number of magazines and became a practicing Presbyterian, Universalist and Unitarian in succession. After he converted to the Unitarian religion he occupied several pulpits in New Hampshire, Vermont and New York and used these opportunities to advance his ideas on social reform. Each time he apparently hoped that he would find a satisfying faith in the new group.

It was during this time that he conceived the idea of his "Church of the Future" which, in his mind, was the utopia of religion. It would

---

*Editor's Note: In this section Orestes Brownson and Isaac Hecker are studied together. Though one served as a layman and the other became a priest, there are many similarities in their lives and in their search for the truth. Isaac Hecker was greatly influenced by Orestes Brownson, yet Brownson became a Catholic after Hecker did. The biographies are separate but the Learning Experiences are designed to apply to both men.

combine the beliefs of Catholics and Protestants so that both could join in one religion.

He also continued his fight against social injustices, but by 1840 he was severely disappointed that so little progress had been made in the way of reform. He lightened his stress on social reforms and began to concentrate on spiritual growth once again. This time his search led him to the Catholic tradition, and in October, 1844, Bishop John Fitzpatrick of Boston received Brownson into the Church. His family followed him— his wife and their eight children—as well as Sophia Ripley, the wife of one of his Transcendentalist* friends, George Ripley.** Brownson felt strongly that Catholics should become involved and act on the social issues and the problems of the times. He decried that even though many Catholics were college graduates, in general they held back from leadership on social reforms or government positions.

James Gibbons, later to become Cardinal Gibbons (see biography), was influenced toward his vocation as a priest after reading Brownson's article about the value of the priesthood in *Review*. Brownson was quite active in political issues. He and President Abraham Lincoln discussed the slavery issue several times. Catholics often met for discussions in his home at Chelsea near Boston.

Because he believed that the layman had a greater role to play in the growing Church, Brownson proposed a "Congress for Laymen" for delegates who were advanced in social thinking, who encouraged the rights of laborers and who stressed the idea of lay involvement. Cardinal Gibbons reluctantly agreed, but the Congress did not actually meet until November 11 and 12, 1889, 13 years after Orestes Brownson's death. Fifteen hundred delegates attended, but the movement did not grow.

When Darwin's theory of biological evolution became the controversial issue of the day, Brownson became involved in the dispute. He refuted the theory but argued that, though science in its present form had its limitations, true science and true religion were harmonious and did not conflict with each other. He strongly encouraged Catholics to become leaders in scientific research to prove the harmony of the two.

By 1857, Brownson was a very ill man. Painful eye inflammations did not keep him from studying late into the night under a kerosene lamp, but there were periods when he suffered temporary blindness. A doctor pronounced his illness as gout of the eyes. When the disease spread to his hands and feet he had to give up lecturing.

---

*Transcendentalism: A philosophy and, in the U.S., a literary, social and religious movement which began in New England among the Unitarians. It reached its peak during the 1840's.

**George Ripley: A literary critic and social reformer who headed the Brook Farm Project near West Roxbury, Massachusetts. It was a farm and a school begun by some Transcendentalists to develop a union between intellectual growth and manual labor.

Later, worsening social conditions caused him to begin "writing" (by dictation) again. Some of his old articles were reprinted and he was again in demand to lecture. In tremendous pain, he was lifted into carriages to take him to the audiences, where he spoke with a halting and unsteady voice. In 1858, a single lecture brought him an audience of 5,376 people and an income of $1,018!

In 1862, some loyal friends provided a lifetime annual annuity of $1,000 because he was unable to continue lecturing. He lived with his daughter, Sarah, with whom he could not get along. His overbearing attitude had alienated him from all his children except for one devoted son, Henry, who was a lawyer in Detroit. Two of his other sons had died in the Civil War.

By now he was a lonely old man, still suffering from gout and half blind, who screamed over the voices of others and who had to have others shout so he could hear. Sarah, nevertheless, cared for him as he became increasingly incapacitated. On Easter Monday, April 17, 1876, he died.

His bodily remains lie in a crypt beneath the center aisle of Sacred Heart Church at Notre Dame University. His ideals remain alive in the volumes of letters and periodicals which are now contained in the Notre Dame Archives, the Massachusetts Historical Society, Harvard College and the New York Public Library.

In his lifetime he wrote and edited several influential periodicals: *Review, Boston Quarterly Review, Brownson's Review, American Republic*. He contributed articles for the Paulists' *Catholic World*. His essay "The Laboring Classes" from the *American Republic* was praised by Arthur Schlesinger as "perhaps the best study of the workings of society written by an American before the Civil War." It still is studied today because of its insight into the issues which led to the Civil War.

Orestes Brownson was an extraordinary man. Self-educated, a master of prose with a keen intellect, single-minded in his pursuit of truth, he persevered until he found a spiritual home that satisfied him. He was sensitive to the poor and laboring classes. He fought against urbanization and "decaying" capitalism. He constantly appealed for lay participation in the Church. All these ingredients wove a continuous thread through his whole complex and controversial life. His literary genius makes him a man not just for Catholics, but for all Americans.

Recommended Readings

Gilhooley, Leonard. *Contradictions and Dilemma: Orestes Brownson and the American Idea.* New York: Fordham University Press, 1972.

Maynard, Theodore. *Orestes Brownson: Yankee Radical, Catholic.* New York: Hafner Press, 1971.

Sveino, Per. *Orestes A. Brownson's Road to Catholicism.* Highlands, New Jersey: Humanities, 1970.

Isaac Hecker (1819-1888)

"I am for accepting the American civilization with its usages and customs; leaving aside other reasons, it is the only way by which Catholicism can become the religion of our people."
— Isaac Hecker

One of the first notable American converts to the Catholic Church in the 19th century was born in New York City on December 18, 1819, the youngest son of German immigrants. As a youngster he often noticed the injustices most workers endured as industrialization grew and by the time he was a teenager he believed that God was calling him to a special mission of correcting social injustice.

His beliefs were reinforced when he heard a tall, fiery man, only 16 years older than he, speaking at a rally in New York City. The man was the Unitarian preacher Orestes Brownson (see biography) and his dedication to the cause of social reform was to have a tremendous influence on Isaac Hecker. Hecker became a disciple of Brownson, totally devoted to his teachings.

While on a speaking engagement, Brownson was invited to stay at the Hecker home. During his three-week visit he talked about his plans for

99

the "Church of the Future." He encouraged young Isaac Hecker to deepen his own beliefs by studying religion and philosophy. After looking into the Episcopal, Congregational, Methodist and Mormon faiths Hecker found himself asking, "What does God desire of me?" He finally decided that prayer and meditation would lead to a specific answer; he felt he had to leave his family and friends and dedicate himself to Christ in a special way.

Alarmed at his behavior, the Hecker family called Brownson in to help the intense young man. Brownson recommended that Isaac sort out his thoughts while living at the Transcendentalist farm near Boston. There, many intellectuals discussed current issues and lived in a simple community style. Isaac accepted Brownson's advice, offered his talent as an expert baker and stayed at Brook Farm for a year with George and Sophia Ripley, Ralph Waldo Emerson, William Ellery Channing and others. Because of his serious search for the truth, he earned the nickname, "Ernest the Seeker."

Brownson, too, had a history of going from one religion to another. Founding his own "Church of the Future" was his last step before he seriously considered joining the Catholic Church. Under Brownson's guidance, Isaac became interested in the Catholic faith and, after attending Mass, he later recalled that he felt, "This is it! This is where I belong!"

He took instructions and was baptized in August, 1844, in St. Patrick's Cathedral by Bishop McCloskey. His brother, George, and his "spiritual father," Orestes Brownson, followed him into the Church a few months later.

Filled with enthusiasm for his newfound faith, Isaac Hecker decided he wanted to become a priest. He felt he should serve God as a missionary in America, and so in September, 1845, he traveled to Belgium to begin his studies at the Redemptorist seminary. Four years later, just before his 30th birthday, he was ordained and after spending a year in England he returned to the United States to begin his missionary work.

Father Hecker, with four fellow Redemptorists, Francis Asbury Baker, Clarence Walworth, George Deshon and Augustine Hewit, all converts to Catholicism, had a tremendous impact on the overflowing crowds of many faiths who came to hear them preach. They were in great demand from New York to Florida to Ohio. In fact, James Gibbons (see biography) heard Father Hecker and Father Walworth preach and later, after reading Brownson's articles in *Review,* he decided to join the priesthood.

At that time most of the work of the Redemptorists in the United States was done by German-speaking missionaries who served the Catholic immigrants from Germany. Hecker and his fellow convert-priests preached to the English-speaking faithful and were convinced of the need for the foundation of a special house for English-speaking missionaries either in New York City or in Newark, New Jersey. In three interviews with their superior Hecker attempted to get approval for this plan. Three times the superior refused permission. In desperation, the priests traveled to Rome to appeal their case. On arrival, they were notified that they were expelled from the Redemptorist Order because they did not have the permission of the Superior General to go.

The incident left Father Hecker brokenhearted. He had never intended for this to happen. He loved his faith, his work and his vocation as a Redemptorist and, when he heard of the decision, he anguished, "I have lost the home of my heart." His appeal to be reinstated in the order was denied.

Pope Pius IX, however, considered his devotion and missionary talents and dispensed Hecker as well as his companions from the Redemptorist vows. Then he requested that Father Hecker establish his own order of American missionaries according to the original concept and he gave the group his blessing.

Overjoyed beyond their wildest dreams, the five priests became the first members of the Missionary Society of Saint Paul the Apostle (Paulist Fathers), the first strictly American congregation in America. For their motto they adopted the words of their patron, Paul, the Apostle of the Gentiles: "One Lord, one faith, one baptism."

The busy and widely acclaimed Paulists filled a tremendous need in America with their continuing work of preaching retreats and missions and administering parishes. Knowing there was more that could be done, Father Hecker recognized the necessity for communicating the faith not only in person, but also through the apostolate of the press. Previously, as a Redemptorist, he had written *Questions of the Soul* and *Aspirations of Nature* as guides to those interested in the Catholic faith. Now, in 1865, he wrote and published his own periodical, *Catholic World,* and in 1870, he began *The Young Catholic,* a magazine for children.

Other Paulist publications spoke out for social justice and the rights of workers and expounded on the virtues of patriotism and freedom; numerous books and pamphlets fearlessly and effectively fought against the charges that Catholics were dangerous to American democracy. Since the establishment of the Paulist Press, hundreds of thousands of inexpensive publications on many faith-related subjects have circulated worldwide.

Father Hecker was one of the most important clerics of his time. In 1866 he was invited to speak at the Second Baltimore Council and advocated greater use of the laity to counteract an idea "on the minds of the public that lay Catholics had nothing to do in their religion."

The impact of Isaac Hecker on America has continued since his death in 1888 through the Paulist priests and the Paulist Press. The Press continues to promote the harmony and interdependence of the Catholic faith and American ideals. Today, the Paulists specialize in radio and television communications, ecumenism, inner-city work and Catholic ministry on secular campuses.

Recommended Readings

Holden, Vincent F., C.S.P. *The Yankee Paul: Isaac Thomas Hecker.* Milwaukee: Bruce, 1958.

McSorley, Joseph. *Isaac Hecker and His Friends.* Paramus, New Jersey: Paulist-Newman, 1972.

Learning Experience
Primary Level

TEACHER NOTES:

After telling the children about Isaac Hecker and Orestes Brownson, focus their attention on how the two men shared their faith by writing newspaper and magazine articles about Jesus' life, about the things Jesus said, and about how much they loved him.

LEARNING EXPERIENCE: Magazine

Suggest that they create a magazine which would be like a messenger bringing "good news" to others to help them know Jesus better. Guide them in a discussion of bible stories and parables they are familiar with and then pass out pieces of paper on which the children can do simple "line drawings" to illustrate the stories they have discussed. Explain that the pictures will be transferred onto another special piece of paper called a ditto master or stencil and then, with the help of a machine, reproduced many times so that many people can read the "good news." Ask for volunteers from the class to help write brief narrations or captions to their illustrations and then, when the work has been mimeographed, encourage them to help with the assembly of their magazine. Give the class an opportunity to vote on a name for their magazine, as well as who should receive copies (families, friends, students).

SUPPLIES:

Stencils or ditto masters.

Learning Experience
Intermediate Level

TEACHER NOTES:

Supply each of the students with a copy of the biographies of Isaac Hecker and Orestes Brownson. Give them time to reflect on the biographies and then pass out construction paper to each student.

LEARNING EXPERIENCE: Road Map

After a brief discussion of the many serious decisions both Brownson and Hecker made during their lifetimes, share these directions with the class:

"Decide whether you would prefer to map out the life of Orestes Brownson or of Isaac Hecker. After you choose one or the other, do a road map of his life by writing in the real choices that the man had to make at different times in his life. Consult the biographies provided, so that you are accurate, and remember that some roads lead to 'dead ends' while others lead to more 'decisions.' You will have 15 minutes."

When everyone has finished, invite individuals to share their solutions with the class. Make sure that both Brownson and Hecker are discussed.

SUPPLIES:

Construction paper for each student, biographies, magic markers, pencils or pens.

Learning Experience
Junior High Level

TEACHER NOTES:

After relating the biographies of Isaac Hecker and Orestes Brownson to the youngsters, draw their attention to the fact that although both men were concerned about many of the same social and religious issues, they chose to explore those issues in distinctly different roles: Isaac Hecker chose to live as a priest and Orestes Brownson chose to live as a layman. Both men, regardless of their different roles, dedicated their lives to educating laypeople about their Church and encouraged laypeople to participate in their Church.

LEARNING EXPERIENCE: Panel Discussion

To bring the youngsters to a deeper awareness of the responsibility of laypeople in a religious community, invite into the class your pastor and several parish council members (including a woman member of the parish council if possible) for a panel discussion of lay participation in the Church. Ask the panel members to discuss lay involvement in the liturgy, religious education, social development projects and financial affairs and to mention, as well, any areas in which the children may share in the ministry of their Church. Be sure to give the youngsters an opportunity to ask questions and to offer their own comments before the panel adjourns.

James Augustine Healy (1830-1900)

"Unless you take up your cross daily and follow me you cannot be my disciple. . . ."

—Luke 14:27

As the spiritual leader of all Catholics in the Portland, Maine, Diocese, America's first Negro bishop, James Augustine Healy, often referred to the biblical passage from Paul to the Colossians, "We are of that church where there is neither Gentile nor Jew, circumcision nor uncircumcision, barbarian nor Scythian, slave nor free man, but Christ is all, and in all." The scriptural passage was especially meaningful to Bishop Healy because he had grown up as a boy of Negro descent in a century when most black men and women knew only the bonds of slavery. Paul's words had been a source of strength and hope which freed him, during a priesthood that spanned 56 years, to build bonds of love that embraced people of every color and economic background.

James Healy's earliest memories were of the rolling clay hills of Jones County, Georgia, where he was born and spent his boyhood with his Irish immigrant father, Michael Healy, his Negro mother, Eliza, and his nine brothers and sisters. The family lived in a rather remote area of the Georgia frontier near the Ocmulgee River on land which Michael Healy shrewdly acquired and managed into a profitable cotton plantation which provided financial security for his family. Unfortunately, Georgia's iron statutes prohibited the legal marriage of his father to his mother, Eliza, who herself had been born a slave, and all of the Healy children were born into absolute and perpetual slavery.

As time passed, neither Michael Healy's vast landholdings and monetary wealth nor his abundant love for his wife and children could secure their freedom from the discrimination of native Georgians. In the autumn

105

of 1837, he traveled to New York City and, with the help of friends and relatives who had emigrated there from Ireland, he undertook a desperate search for a school in the northern free states that would educate his swarthy-skinned, bushy-haired youngsters in an environment free of insinuation about their mixed parentage. He found a Quaker school in Flushing, New York, that would accept them. Unfortunately, although administrators of the school patronized the ideals of brotherly love, the students with whom James and his brothers were in constant contact did not uphold the school's traditions when it came to the "boys from Georgia." The Healy brothers were bracketed with racial slurs because of their Negro blood, on one hand, and scorned because of their immigrant Irish Catholic ancestry, on the other.

Even though the education James received at the Quaker school was invaluable, the painful separation from his family and the bitter racial prejudice of his peers had wounded him deeply. Michael Healy was fully aware of the hardship his children were enduring but it wasn't until he met Bishop John Fitzpatrick of Boston on a boat ride up the Atlantic Coast that an alternative plan emerged to relieve their suffering. Aboard ship, Healy related to Bishop Fitzpatrick the problems of his family's separation and his deep concern for his children's welfare. The Bishop was moved by the story and immediately suggested a plan to make their future more promising. The prelate convinced Michael Healy to enroll James, Hugh, Patrick and Sherwood in Holy Cross College in Worcester, Massachusetts, and even arranged for James' sister, Martha, to live with members of his own family in Boston while she attended the Notre Dame Sisters' school there.

Although neither Eliza nor Michael Healy ever permanently left the Georgia plantation before their deaths in 1850, all of the surviving Healy children left their birthplace to be educated outside the slave states. Throughout his lifetime James kept in contact with all his brothers and sisters through frequent reunions. He maintained an especially close relationship with his brother, Sherwood, who became a highly respected Catholic priest in the Boston Diocese, and Patrick, who became a Jesuit and eventually president of Georgetown University.

The stimulating atmosphere of the classes at Holy Cross gave James an opportunity to develop his natural abilities for philosophy, history and literature. The Jesuits and the inspiring religious experience made him acutely aware of his own deep faith and the ministry into which he was being called to share his special talents.

James graduated first in his class and entered the Sulpician Seminary in Montreal to study for the priesthood. Difficulties arose just as he was about to receive his minor orders in 1850, however, when he was not able to produce the necessary documents to prove his parents' marriage and his legitimacy. He appealed to Bishop Fitzpatrick and a dispensation was granted within a year. In 1852, James transferred to the Sulpician Seminary in France where he continued his brilliant record. His seminary years there were, nevertheless, marred by his constant fear of being someday unaccepted and perhaps ineffective as a priest in white Catholic communities because of his race. As a possible solution he had even seriously considered the refuge of an academic teaching position in a secluded religious order.

However, shortly after his ordination in 1854, while accompanying Bishop Fitzpatrick and a friend on a trip into the Paris slums to observe rehabilitation of poverty victims, James Healy's fears were subdued by the desperate cries of needy children. The degenerate condition of the Paris slums had awakened a social consciousness in the newly ordained Father Healy. Reflecting on the richness of his own experience and for the first time seeing his vocation clearly in terms of the needs of others, he boldly met the challenge of an apostolate among the poor.

Boston's Irish immigrant poor accepted him and gave him assurance. Young boys in an orphans' home and the Irish immigrants of a ghetto community in Bishop Fitzpatrick's Boston Diocese were Father Healy's first flock. In the hope of relieving their suffering, he daily faced contagion from smallpox, tuberculosis and typhus in their disease-ridden hovels. In spite of the gathering storm of discontent over the slave issue in the states, these parishioners found consolation in his personal holiness, burning compassion and warm friendship.

The dauntless zeal which characterized Father Healy's ministry that year gained him a reputation as a champion for the underprivileged. In particular, his efforts drew the attention of the Most Reverend John Fitzpatrick who recognized his special gifts of leadership and arranged for a series of specific assignments to foster their development.

Within a year Bishop Fitzpatrick transferred Father Healy to the cathedral staff where he was given the task of establishing the first chancery office in the diocese. Although the job was enormous, Father Healy was equal to the task and he performed his administrative duties well. During the same period, he gained a reputation as an eloquent homilist. Bishop Fitzpatrick encouraged his protégé to preach regularly in the cathedral in Boston and often sent him out to speak at ordinations and other special occasions elsewhere in the diocese.

By the time of Bishop Fitzpatrick's death in 1866, Father James Healy was acknowledged as one of the foremost Catholic clergymen in New England. As Bishop Fitzpatrick had perceived so many years before, no challenge seemed too great for this extraordinary priest. Father Healy's dedication to the underprivileged in the following decade never ceased.

As Deputy to the Social Apostolate for the Boston Diocese, he played a decisive part in establishing many charitable organizations and institutions to aid destitute Catholic children. In the wider civic community, Father Healy actively contributed to the organization of the first Catholic Labor Union in Boston. Working closely with local labor leaders, he diligently sought to secure equal opportunity for scores of disenfranchised immigrants who were victimized by unjust laws.

Father Healy's inspiring spiritual leadership and pioneering efforts to secure equal rights for the underprivileged were rewarded with his appointment as bishop of Portland, Maine. His sprawling diocese contained only 10 permanent church buildings when he arrived, but in the next 25 years his continued resourcefulness enabled it to multiply sixfold. Stories from the rich Church lore of Portland, however, reveal the warm and amiable relationship Bishop James Healy had with his flock far more poignantly than the statistical accomplishments of his reign.

Even to this day memories of the beloved Bishop Healy racing through the streets of Portland in his horse-drawn sleigh, pulling a train of happy children on sleds behind him, are fondly recalled. Tales of his ice-skating with youngsters in winter or strolling with children at his coattails in summer are vividly retold as well. His frequent visits to foundling homes and schools and his horseback rides through the streets with saddlebags of provisions for the sick and poor of his diocese are also colorfully portrayed.

On August 5, 1900, James Augustine Healy died, a victim of heart failure, and, in accordance with his expressed will, he was buried in a Catholic cemetery among the flock he so dearly loved. The diaries and letters he left offer us a glimpse of the humble, prayerful, compassionate man so often alluded to in the Church legends of Portland. But the many churches, schools and welfare institutions which continue 100 years later to serve with genuine care and concern for the dignity of each man and woman in this country reveal more precisely the greatness of this American Catholic.

Recommended Readings

Foley, Albert S., S.J. *Bishop Healy: Beloved Outcast.* New York: Arno Press, 1970. (American Negro: His History and Literature Series, # 3)

Foley, Albert S. *God's Men of Color.* New York: Arno Press, 1969. (American Negro: His History and Literature Series, #2)

Learning Experience
Primary Level

TEACHER NOTES:
After telling the children the story of James Augustine Healy, review the major events in his life by pointing out on a map the places where he was born (Georgia) and educated (New York, New Jersey, Massachusetts), the areas where he worked as a priest (Massachusetts), and as a bishop (Maine). In the course of your review, ask them why they think he was called by many people then (and is remembered even today) as the "Children's Bishop."

LEARNING EXPERIENCE: Collage

Give each of the youngsters a large (2' x 2') precut, poster board "heart," scissors, old magazines, magic markers and paper and paste and ask them to make a collage of pictures, symbols and drawings which remind them of the many ways Bishop Healy shared himself with children (and grown-ups, too) in his lifetime.

SUPPLIES:

Precut poster board "heart," scissors, old magazines, magic markers, paper and paste.

Learning Experience
Intermediate Level

TEACHER NOTES:

When the youngsters have had time to reflect on the biography of Bishop James Augustine Healy, guide them in a discussion of his life by asking why they think he specifically requested to be buried in a cemetery among his flock, rather than in a special place such as a crypt, often reserved in our society for the remains of prominent people. After all the youngsters have had a chance to respond to the question, explain to them that clergymen, parishioners and even children in his diocese in Portland *did* eventually contribute funds for the raising of a memorial to Bishop Healy. Because of his Irish ancestry, a tall Celtic cross was selected to mark his gravesite.

LEARNING EXPERIENCE: Monument

Challenge the youngsters to suggest as many words or phrases as they can think of in two minutes to describe Bishop Healy, his life and his work. Record their suggestions on the blackboard, and then ask them to design and create a replica of a "monument" they feel would appropriately mark the site where he was *born* in Georgia. Give them an ample amount of clay to create their "monument" and tell them to use the words they suggested earlier to describe Bishop Healy as a guide in selecting the form, structure and inscription for the "monument." If possible use clay which will harden after drying or firing so that the youngsters can keep their creation to remind them of this very humble but great American Catholic.

SUPPLIES:

Newspapers to protect desks, tables, floor, and clay (type which will harden after drying or firing).

Learning Experience
Junior High Level

TEACHER NOTES:

When the students have had time to explore the biography of James Augustine Healy, draw them into a discussion about his life by asking questions such as the following:

- Why were Eliza and Michael Healy not permitted to marry in the state of Georgia in the early part of the 19th century?
- Why did James Healy and his brothers and sisters have to go to the northern states to be educated?
- What were some of the hardships he endured while he was in school?
- What were some of the fears he harbored during his seminary and priestly life? Why?

LEARNING EXPERIENCES: Litany

Despite the personal suffering James Healy endured in his lifetime because of discrimination, he dedicated his ministry to relieving suffering in the lives of the poor and the oppressed. Even though over 100 years later his dream of equal justice for all people had not come true, it was in the 1960's hopefully reaffirmed. Martin Luther King said then, "I have a dream that my four little children will one day live in a nation where they will not be judged by the color of their skin but by the content of their character." Ask the students today to reflect prayerfully on their own dreams for the future and to express those dreams in a litany of faith and hope. Provide the youngsters with paper and pencils, ask them to work individually or in groups to write a litany and then give them time to share their hopes and dreams together in prayer before the end of the class. Suggest that they use the form:

"I have a dream that. . . .

. . . . . LORD HELP ME TO MAKE IT COME TRUE."

SUPPLIES:

Paper, pencils.

James Cardinal Gibbons (1834-1921)

". . . single-minded patriotism and love of country on the one hand, and sincere devotion to his church and God upon the other."
— William Howard Taft, U.S. President

No one could better appreciate the cause of the immigrant and the workingman than James Gibbons. Born to Irish immigrants on July 23, 1834, in Baltimore, Maryland, he became America's second cardinal and one of the greatest American spokesmen for the Catholic Church.

James' father, Thomas, had done well in the new land and had prospered as a clerk for an importing business. His health failed, however, and the doctor's orders for a sea voyage sent the family from Baltimore to County Mayo in Ireland where they lived for 16 years.

James began his education in Ireland and learned Latin, Greek and English. Besides being a model student with a deep love for books, he was a well-rounded youngster who enjoyed cricket, handball, swimming and was a champion at marbles. He also served Mass at St. Mary's Church in Ballinrobe.

In Ireland, James knew poverty in the fullest sense of the word, because his family endured the crop failure, famine and epidemic of the 1840's which took the lives of his father and his sister Catherine. The remainder of the Gibbons family joined 218,000 Irish in 1853 to journey to America, their new hope for the future.

Since his mother, Bridget, could not bear the memories of the earlier years in Baltimore, the family chose New Orleans as their new home. But the trials were not over. After working as a grocery clerk there, James contracted yellow fever and was nursed from near death by his oldest sister, Mary. He always remained frail after his slow recovery.

When he was 19 years old, James attended a ten-day mission conducted by the Redemptorist priests (see biography of Isaac Hecker) and in further study he read the works of Orestes Brownson (see biography) in *Review*. As a result, his vocation became clear and he chose to become a Sulpician priest in the Diocese of Baltimore, where he earned outstanding grades in the seminary.

At the time of his ordination, the country was steeped in the Civil War and, though his brother fought for the Confederacy, his own loyalty remained with the Union. As a new 27-year-old priest, his first assignment was with St. Patrick's Church, which was located in a waterfront section of Baltimore. Six weeks later he was reassigned as pastor of St. Bridget's Church in Mt. Savage, Maryland, where his parishioners were very poor industrial workers from copper works and agricultural workers from small farms.

It was not unusual then for workers to work 18 hours a day, six days a week for $6.00 per week. Each day was a fight for survival. Father Gibbons' own living quarters reflected the poverty of his parish: a small lean-to built against the church with no light or ventilation and only floorboards on the ground.

Less than a year later, as an added burden, he became pastor of a second church, St. Lawrence O'Toole, a parish of poor dockworkers and shipbuilders. The work was very strenuous and his condition became more frail as he traveled back and forth across the river between the two parishes each Sunday while observing the midnight Communion fast. This dual assignment and his run-down condition caused him to suffer a digestive ailment which would plague him the rest of his life. Besides serving the two parishes, Father Gibbons volunteered as chaplain at Fort Marshall and Fort McHenry during the Civil War and ministered to Union soldiers and Confederate prisoners alike.

Father Gibbons rose quickly in the ranks of the priesthood. After the Civil War Archbishop Spalding assigned Gibbons to work as his secretary. When the plans were made for holding the Second Plenary Council in October, 1866, Father Gibbons became assistant chancellor of the council.

Father Gibbons' work did not go unnoticed. The attending bishops saw the piety, leadership and administrative ability of the 34-year-old priest and in 1868 successfully recommended him to Rome to become the Vicar Apostolic of a new diocese in Wilmington, North Carolina. Father Gibbons preferred not to leave his beloved Baltimore, but obeyed the call. With only a few priests in his whole new diocese, the responsibility for the vast 50,000-square-mile state with its widely scattered 700 Catholics was staggering. Yet within five days after his arrival the new bishop baptized the first convert. Travels within his diocese brought him in contact with people of many faiths, not only through talks in churches of different denominations but also in town halls. He had an appealing way of explaining the faith in warm, clear and interesting language. As a result, many people embraced Catholicism.

In 1876, to explain Catholic doctrine in simple terms, he wrote *Faith of Our Fathers,* almost two million copies of which were printed, in ten editions and several languages. Thirteen years later, his second book, *Our Christian Heritage,* won widespread acclaim, as also did a third book written for priests.

In 1869, Bishop Gibbons attended the First Vatican Council in Rome with Archbishop Spalding. When the Bishop of Richmond died in 1872, Bishop Gibbons was given the added responsibility of that see. He worked to serve both dioceses well, and by 1877 he was appointed Archbishop of Baltimore which at that time encompassed Maryland and the District of Columbia and was considered the "capital of the American Church."

One of the biggest problems Gibbons had to face was the massive wave of immigrants. The government depended on the churches to handle the health, education and welfare of the people in their own parishes, so the archbishop expanded the parochial school system to Americanize the immigrants as well as educate them in faith and academics. Hospitals, homes for the aged and orphanages sprang up to fill the growing needs of the people.

To further advance education he sought permission from Rome in 1888 to found the Catholic University of America. With Pope Leo XIII's approval, Caldwell Hall was dedicated with President Cleveland, Theodore Roosevelt and Benjamin Harrison attending. Bishop Gibbons was the first chancellor. When it became evident that the parochial schools could not handle the increasing student population, he supported the public schools, too, and asked that religion be taught after class time in the schools. This was a point of controversy among many bishops.

Gibbons became the confidant of several presidents who appreciated his cooperation, tact, patriotism and sound judgment. They turned to him on personal, local and international matters. President McKinley asked for his advice in the handling of Puerto Rico and the Philippines during the Spanish-American War.

In the late 1800's a depression rocked the national economic foundations, casting the jobless into deeper poverty and the employed into deplorable working conditions with equally deplorable wages. As a united front against these injustices, the *Knights of Labor* was organized. Names of the members were kept secret to prevent them from being fired by their employers. Bishops John Ireland and John Keane backed the organization, and by 1885 there were more than 71,000 members in this first major American labor organization. But several bishops were suspicious of any secret organization and they recommended condemnation of the Knights. After careful investigation, however, Cardinal Gibbons stood firm in defense of the Knights not only before the American bishops, but also in personal conversations with Pope Leo XIII in Rome. Four years later

Pope Leo wrote the encyclical *Rerum Novarum,* defending the rights of workingmen to form unions and to work for just wages.

So much was Cardinal Gibbons respected that on his silver jubilee as bishop in 1893 Baltimore honored him with a civic celebration. On June 6, 20,000 persons arrived to honor him at the Fifth Regiment Armory. Government dignitaries came from all over the United States. A special train from Washington brought President Taft, Vice President James Sherman, Speaker of the House of Representatives, Champ Clark and others. Chief Justice Edward White arrived from New Orleans. Ambassadors, senators and countless other dignitaries showered mountains of praise on him for his contributions to Church and government. The gentle, unassuming cardinal, very moved, replied, ". . . I have become so enamored of your portrait that it shall be the endeavor of my life to imitate and resemble that portrait more and more during the few years that remain to me in this world" (*The Life of James Cardinal Gibbons* by Tracy Ellis).

During his golden jubilee year as a priest in 1911, he helped two priests, Father Thomas Price and Father James Walsh, found an American Missionary Society to serve in foreign countries. With Rome's approval, the Catholic Foreign Mission Society of America (Maryknoll) took root, and Father Price and three other priests left to serve China, and later, the rest of the Orient.

As a person, Cardinal Gibbons was a priestly man whose whole lifestyle was simplicity itself. He profoundly loved and respected others and his door at 408 North Charles Street was always open to all. He had a good sense of humor; he never lacked courage to face an unpleasant issue, yet he remained unruffled in the most unsettling circumstances. His patriotism and loyalty were cherished values and they surfaced continually during the dark times of the Civil War, the Spanish-American War and the First World War, or at any time a President called on him for cooperation or assistance. His keen, perceptive mind, his sense of excellent judgment and tactful manner raised high the status of the American Catholic Church.

In 1917, President Theodore Roosevelt told the cardinal: "Taking your life as a whole, I think you now occupy the position of being the most respected, and venerated and useful citizen of our country."

These words rang true, for when James Cardinal Gibbons died on March 24, 1921, at 87 years he was mourned worldwide. Today the American Church retains many of the ideals of this crusader for the social gospel who made the Church a haven for the oppressed and who welcomed the fellowship of all.

Recommended Readings

Ellis, John Tracy. *The Life of James Cardinal Gibbons, Archbishop of Baltimore 1834-1921.* Milwaukee: Bruce, 1963.

Greeley, Andrew. *The Catholic Experience.* Garden City, New York: Doubleday, Image Books, 1967.

Learning Experience
Primary Level

TEACHER NOTES:

After you have told the children the story of Cardinal Gibbons, discuss some of the major events in his life with them, and invite them to act out those events in a play about him.

LEARNING EXPERIENCE: Play

Encourage all the youngsters in the class to participate in the play, provide them with simple props (such as name tags, hats, dress-ups) and tell them that you would like them to act out the story in "pantomime" while you narrate it.

SUPPLIES:

Props, play.

THE LIFE OF JOHN CARDINAL GIBBONS

CHARACTERS:

Mother, father, sister, James, doctor, poor people, prisoners, soldiers, pope, President Taft, Vice-President, senators, important people.

SCENE I:

James is born in Baltimore and when he is just a small boy, his father becomes very sick. The doctor tells the family that his father must take a long ocean voyage to get well. The family travels on a ship to Ireland and lives on a farm as James grows up. James helps his parents with the farming, goes to school, and enjoys swimming and playing marbles in his free time. After a few years the family is starving because the vegetables on the farm will not grow very well. His father and sister get sick and die. James' Mother is very sad and tells the rest of the family that they must go back to America to live.

SCENE II:

James grows up and decides to serve the people in this country by becoming a priest, "Father Gibbons." Many poor people come to him for help because they are sick and hungry and don't have jobs, but Father Gibbons cannot help them very much because he is very poor too. During the Civil War he visits the sad prisoners and soldiers in the nearby fort and they are very happy to see him.

SCENE III:

Father Gibbons becomes a bishop and now has even more poor people to serve. He works very hard to help them and encourages many other people to help them as well. He has workers build schools to help the poor people learn to read and write, and hospitals to help them get well when they are sick. Bishop Gibbons is very wise and even the President asks for his help when he has a problem.

SCENE IV:

Bishop Gibbons is now given another new name, Cardinal Gibbons. As a Cardinal he leads many more people to help poor families live a happier life. He encourages fathers who only make one dollar for a whole day's work to join together in a special club so that they can ask for fair pay together in one big voice, rather than in many small voices. Many fathers now have enough money to buy food, to pay the rent and to pay for clothes to keep their families warm. He visits the pope in Rome and tells him about the people in America. The pope is very happy to see Cardinal Gibbons help the poor in America.

SCENE V:

When Cardinal Gibbons had served the people for 25 years as their leader, the President and the Vice-President of the United States, senators and many, many other people had a great celebration to show him how much they loved him. Many of the important people who came to the celebration told in speeches about the wonderful things Cardinal Gibbons did for others. Even today he is remembered as a great man who loved and served others . . . the best he could!

Learning Experience
Intermediate Level

TEACHER NOTES:

Give the youngsters an opportunity to reflect on the life of John Cardinal Gibbons and then ask them a few pertinent questions, in order to focus their attention on the plight of the poor immigrant workingmen when James Gibbons first came in contact with them after he was ordained a priest:

- Where did most of the immigrants live when they first came to this country?
- What kind of jobs did they have? What was it like where they worked? About how much money did they make?
- Did they have enough money to feed, clothe and educate their families?

LEARNING EXPERIENCE: Fact-finding Mission
Tell the youngsters that in the next week you would like them to go on a fact-finding mission to seek "concrete evidence" that the living and working conditions of the workingman have truly improved in the past century. Tell them to search for pictures and articles describing conditions *before* the organization of labor and challenge them to use their own cameras to take pictures of working conditions and living conditions of laborers in their communities *today*. When they present their "evidence" give them time to share their own "facts" and explore those gathered by the other members of the class.

SUPPLIES:
Paper, pencils, several inexpensive cameras, film.

Learning Experience
Junior High Level

TEACHER NOTES:
When the students have had sufficient time to review the information in the biography about John Cardinal Gibbons, ask them to think for a few moments, did Cardinal Gibbons' life "make a difference" to people in the last century and if so why?

LEARNING EXPERIENCE: Banner
After the students have responded to the question and commented on one another's thoughts, separate them into groups of three or four and ask them to show *how* he did or did not "make a difference" in the lives of many Americans living and working in the last century. Pass out a large piece of burlap, scraps of colored yarn and cloth and several large crewel needles to each group and ask them to "stitch" scenes, words and symbols onto the banner to highlight the concerns Cardinal Gibbons expressed and the activities in which he was involved throughout his lifetime.

SUPPLIES:
One large piece of burlap per group for banner, one large crewel needle per student, yarn in a variety of colors and widths, scraps of cloth (to create an embroidered effect).

Paraliturgical Celebration for Unit III
Era of Expansion and Industrialization

Theme:

Today's liturgy celebrates the special contributions of five people: Pierre-Jean DeSmet, Orestes Brownson, Isaac Hecker, James Augustine Healy and James Cardinal Gibbons, who knew that it is not enough merely to listen to the message of the gospel, but that each person must *act* on that message once it has been heard. Because each of them recognized the dignity of all persons, but especially of our native Americans and the immigrants, they were not afraid to speak out against the injustices they saw. These faith-filled men lived during the 19th century and, because they heard the gospel message and really believed it, they worked hard to make this country become a better place.

Entrance Hymn:

"Faith of Our Fathers," *Worship,* G.I.A.

Youngsters carrying large symbols of each of the five men studied in this unit accompany the celebrant while everybody is singing the entrance song. In addition, one student could carry a banner with the words, "Act on the Message," and then place it where all can see it.

Suggestions for symbols:

Pierre-Jean DeSmet . . . Indian blanket, folded. (Possibly use as a banner during the liturgy.)

Orestes Brownson . . . Large placard made of poster-board with the names of your parish council members listed.

Isaac Hecker . . . Any Paulist Press publication, for example, *Catholic World.*

James Augustine Healy . . . Symbols of children or a drawing of a bishop's miter with the words, "The Children's Bishop," written on it.

James Cardinal Gibbons . . . Symbols of a working person — tools, lunchbox, uniforms, etc.

Penitential Rite:

For the times we found excuses for being unkind to people who are a different color or who speak a different language, Lord, have mercy.

LORD, HAVE MERCY.

120

For not doing something about those who are poorer than we, Christ, have mercy.

CHRIST, HAVE MERCY.

For the courage to make this world a better place to live, Lord, have mercy.

LORD, HAVE MERCY.

First Reading:
Galatians 5:1, 13-15

Gospel Reading:
Matthew 25: 31-40

Homily:
Commenting on the faith of each of these five persons and on how each one heard the message of the gospel and then acted on it in a different way according to his talents. Help the youngsters to make the connection that we, too, are called to make a difference in this world by the way we use our abilities to act on the message of the gospel.

Song:
"All the Earth," Lucien Deiss, *People's Mass Book,* W.L.P.; "Look Beyond the Bread You Eat," Darryl Ducote, *Tell the World,* F.E.L.; "O Lord, With Wondrous Mystery," *People's Mass Book Missal,* W.L.P.

Meditation:
James 1:22-25 "Act on the Message."

Recessional:
"America," *Worship,* G.I.A.

UNIT IV

Toward a New Social Awareness

123

Frances Xavier Cabrini (1850-1917)

"I can do all things in him who strengthens me . . ."
— Saint Paul

In the little town of San Angelo, Italy, Agostino Cabrini was known as the "Christian tower." He was a simple farmer who never ventured beyond the plains surrounding his town, yet his joyful acceptance of the domestic rituals of rural life and his dedicated service to his fellowman were a reminder to the whole community that God was the source of all life and that in living both "the hard and happy times," there was cause for celebration.

No one was more inspired by his words and deeds than the last of his 13 children, Frances. Because she was frail and sickly throughout her childhood, she had been in many ways touched by her father's gentle care very early and began to pattern her own life after his. When on cold winter evenings her father would read to the family from the *Annals of the Propagation of the Faith* accounts of people who had fearlessly lived and died for others, Frances was the most astute listener. She became enthralled by the adventures of the saints and even before she was 13 years old she expressed a burning desire to share her faith as many of them had done in far-off China.

Agostino Cabrini and his wife Stella were aware of their daughter's passion to be a missionary but both feared that her dream of spreading the Good News beyond their homeland would remain hopelessly unfilled. Nevertheless, Frances persevered through one illness after another to achieve her goal. Aware that she would need a firm educational background as a missionary, she studied hard, at first under the tutelage of her sister and then at the Daughters of the Sacred Heart Academy in Arluno, Italy, where at 18 she graduated with highest honors and obtained a license to teach school. Feeling certain even then of her religious vocation, she requested admittance into a religious order but was rejected because of her poor health. For the next few years, although she never dismissed the thought of becoming a religious, she devoted all her time to her aging parents and the chronically ill of her own village. With the death of her parents in 1870, and after a personal bout with smallpox, her determination to become a missionary intensified. She decided to teach for a short time in hope that she would gain experience for use in the missionary field. After accepting a teaching position in the nearby village of Vivardo, she was drawn into teaching religion classes in the Catholic church there under the supervision of the pastor, Father Antonio Serrati. It was not long before Father Serrati recognized Frances' outstanding teaching capabilities, her deep spirituality and her genuine call to missionary life.

While at Vivardo, she continued to apply for admittance into a religious order, but Father Serrati was so concerned about her recurrent illness that without her knowledge he "arranged" for her to be refused. However, when he was transferred to a new assignment in Codogno, he saw an opportunity for Frances' physical and spiritual strength to be put to a profound test under his watchful eye. In addition to a parish, Father Serrati's new assignment included an orphanage for girls called the House of Providence. It was supervised by two lay women religious who lived on the premises. When it became apparent to Father Serrati that the orphanage was not being kept clean and that perhaps the young girls living there were being mistreated, Father called on his good friend, Frances Cabrini, to reform the institution. Explaining that it was a formidable challenge which could prove her fitness for the missionary life, he persuaded her to take on the task for "just two weeks!"

The two weeks stretched into six years and even then Frances Cabrini's strong will could not transform the orphanage into a healthy environment for the homeless girls. Although she had taken on the habit of a lay woman religious during her stay there, improved the sanitary conditions, and provided religious instruction and spiritual guidance to the girls, her attempts to reform the two women had clearly failed.

In 1880, Frances finally met with the bishop of the diocese to admit her own defeat and to make a full disclosure of the two women's activities. Besides their complete disregard for the physical environment of the home, they had repeatedly abused the girls and were deliberately funneling parish funds intended for the maintenance of the orphanage into their own pockets. The bishop was enormously impressed with the personal self-sacrifice Frances had made and, to her surprise, rather than admonish her for her failure to convert the two corrupt women, he rewarded her very valuable contributions by granting her permission to begin her own religious order. With seven of the orphanage girls she had ministered to at the House of Providence as her first novices, that same year Frances Cabrini founded the Missionary Sisters of the Sacred Heart.

In the next seven years, Frances Cabrini inspired many new novices with her missionary zeal. By laying brick and mortar with her own hands she established seven houses in Italy through which teaching and charitable activities for the needy were conducted. By 1887, she realized that the "daughters" she had gathered and nurtured were ready to minister to the needy in foreign lands and she was determined to set up an institute in Rome to serve as headquarters for their missionary work. Prominent clergymen throughout Italy tried to dissuade her from seeking Vatican approval for such a venture and urged her to be content to labor in her own homeland. Even her beloved Father Serrati advised, "These superhuman crosses and ventures we shall appropriately leave to *saints.*"

Indeed they had all underestimated the "saintly" Frances Cabrini! Undaunted by their discouragement, Mother Cabrini, as she was affectionately called by members of her order, packed her bags and set out to convince the powers in Rome to approve of her "mission" abroad. From sunup to sundown, Frances knocked on doors and wrote letters trying to rally support for her project until finally her patience and persistence drew the attention of a cardinal at the Vatican who arranged for Pope Leo XIII to examine the rule of her order and her plans for their missionary work abroad. On March 12, 1888, the Institute she had hoped for was approved and an audience with the Pope was arranged.

Although for years, Frances Cabrini had envisioned herself and her "daughters" carrying God's word to people in the Far East, developments in America in the 19th century were to beckon her instead. A great demand for labor had been created in America's tremendous expansion of industry and technology. In the late 1880's poor disillusioned farmers from Italy's southern districts had become a prime source for that labor. With hopes of benefiting from the riches of America, thousands of Italians had already crossed the Atlantic and were struggling for survival there when Mother Cabrini met with Pope Leo about her missionary assignment. Expressing his deep concern for the fate of Italian immigrants suffering in the squalor of urban slums, the Pope strongly urged Frances and her community to abandon their plans for missionary work in China to aid their countrymen in America.

Bishop Giovanni Battista Scalabrini of Piacenza, Italy, who had in 1877 founded a religious order of priests dedicated to helping Italian immigrants in America, reaffirmed Pope Leo's plea and pledged the support of the priests in his order to assist her in her missionary endeavors. Frances was convinced by Pope Leo and Bishop Scalabrini of the urgent need in America and she began at once to send instructions to each of her houses in Italy to prepare for missionary work in the United States.

With six members of her order, Mother Cabrini arrived in New York City on March 31, 1889, expecting to be greeted at the dock by a representative of the Scalabrinian Fathers or Archbishop Corrigan of New York. On the contrary, only huge concrete structures, hurrying horse-drawn carriages and a mass of humanity completely indifferent to their presence lay before them. They muddled the streets until a policeman directed them to San Gioacchino Church on Randolph Street, but there they met with a greater disillusionment. The Scalabrinian Fathers were not expecting them and, in fact, because of some difficulties over location, the orphanage they were to take over had not yet even been built.

Neither the dismal news concerning facilities for their mission nor their first night in New York City (fighting off arrogant mice in a sleazy hotel room) would dissuade the Missionary Sisters of the Sacred Heart from pursuing their goal. Early the next morning Mother Cabrini appeared at Archbishop Corrigan's residence and adamantly proclaimed, "We have a mission in America ordained by Pope Leo XIII and in America we will stay!"

The Archbishop temporarily assigned the Missionary Sisters of the Sacred Heart to the Parish of San Gioacchino but because Frances Cabrini believed they must minister to the "entire community of Italian immigrants," she immediately broadened the scope of their apostolate to include everyone in the cluttered section of the city called "Little Italy." Each day, as she gallantly led them into the crowded tenements, she reminded the nuns who accompanied her to "Observe unflinchingly the realities of that which causes want, pain, misunderstanding and tragedy. Let us put courageous and probing hands to these injustices and social wounds inflicted upon our dear good people. To grapple with their many problems, we must be close to them. We must keep in close contact with the evil sores of this earth."

Throngs of adult immigrants anxious to renew their faith attended her evening religion classes and enrolled their children in her school. Ignorance of the English language, poor educational background and the many political, social and regional prejudices they had brought with them from Italy were contributing to the immigrants' exploitation in America. The Missionary Sisters and the Scalabrinian Fathers made every effort to offer educational opportunities and a chance for the community to grow spiritually in renewed celebration of the sacraments. Unfortunately, the miserable housing conditions, which alone bred immorality and violence, presented a far more complex problem. Mother Cabrini realized that the problems required an economic as well as a social solution. She knew that there must be a redirecting of the money earned by the immigrants into areas and institutions to serve their welfare, if they were ever to be truly woven into the fabric of American life. She soon became a shrewd businesswoman who was never beyond begging or borrowing to finance her missionary endeavors on their behalf!

By 1891 fifty members of the Missionary Sisters of the Sacred Heart were ministering to immigrants through schools, orphanages, convents and a hospital Mother Cabrini had founded in New York City. Then she decided it was time they extended their services to the needy in Central and South America. Continuing her whirlwind pace she established houses in Nicaragua, Panama, Brazil and Argentina. When satisfied that each house was capable of performing missionary tasks on its own, she moved on to found other houses. Despite respiratory illness and attacks of malaria, she planted houses in Denver, Seattle, New Orleans, Los Angeles and even in cities in England, France and Spain.

It wasn't until December 22, 1917, at the age of 67, and after she had established 67 houses of her sisterhood that Frances Cabrini finally succumbed to severe illness.

When congratulated on her remarkable achievements Frances Cabrini would humbly remark, "I have not done it, God has done it all. I have merely looked on." Although until she was an adult she was not able to read English or fully understand the principles or ideals on which America was founded, in the space of 20 years Mother Cabrini came to appreciate those ideals and express her dedication to them as a citizen of the United States and an American Catholic. In 1946, because of her extraordinary efforts on behalf of thousands of desperate men, women and children, she became the first American citizen to be canonized a saint.

Recommended Readings

DiDonato, Pietro. *Immigrant Saint: The Life of Mother Cabrini.* New York: McGraw-Hill, 1960.

Keyes, Frances Parkinson. *Mother Cabrini, Missionary to the World.* New York: Farrar, Straus & Giroux, 1961.

Learning Experience
Primary Level

TEACHER NOTES:

Once you have related the biography of Mother Cabrini to the children, talk with them about those people who played important parts in her life. Make a list of the people on the blackboard.

LEARNING EXPERIENCE: Puppets

When the children are familiar with the important events in her life and can identify the important people she was associated with, pass out materials with which they can create simple puppets to represent those important people. Encourage the children to make as many puppets as they like and allow enough time for groups of four or five children to engage in simple storytelling with the puppets they have created. Encourage the youngsters to create puppets representing: Francesca Cabrini, her father, her sister, Father Serrati, the two lay women religious at the House of Providence, the orphaned girls, Pope Leo XIII, Bishop Scalabrini, Bishop Corrigan, the Scalabrinian Fathers, sisters of her order.

If the children wish to present a more formal "puppet show" about the life of Mother Cabrini, have several groups tell the story in "segments" and involve as many childern as possible in the production.

SUPPLIES:
Materials for "popsicle stick" puppets (construction paper, scissors, crayons, tape). "Paper bag" puppets would be equally as effective in this learning experience (crayons, paste, scissors, construction paper and "lunch size" brown paper bags).

Learning Experience
Intermediate Level

TEACHER NOTES:
After you have presented the biography of Mother Cabrini to the youngsters, guide them in a discussion exploring the reasons why Italian immigrants left their native land to seek a new life.

LEARNING EXPERIENCE: Letter
Ask half the class to imagine that they are members of an Italian family that moved in the summer of 1890 to New York City from a small farm in southern Italy. Tell them to write a letter to a friend or relative in Italy explaining what it's like in this new land and advising them about whether or not to take the trip themselves.

Ask the other half of the class to imagine that they are Irish immigrants who have lived in America for 10 years. Tell them to write a letter to a friend or relative in Ireland describing their work, living conditions and impressions of the "new Italian immigrant family which, in the summer of 1890, has moved in next door."

When the youngsters have finished their work, encourage them to share what they have written. End the class with a discussion of the problems faced by immigrants settling in America in the 19th century and how their experiences are different or similar to those of immigrants coming to live in this country today.

SUPPLIES:
Paper, pencils.

Learning Experience
Junior High Level

TEACHER NOTES:

After the students have explored the biography of Mother Cabrini, talk with them for a few moments about the unique language, cultural and religious heritage the Italian immigrants brought with them to this country. Invite their thoughts about what factors influenced many Italian immigrants to abandon traditional customs and religious practices in an effort to become "Americanized."

LEARNING EXPERIENCE: "Identity Day"

Have the students do some research on their own cultural heritage by asking the oldest member of their family for information about their ancestors, if possible at least five or six generations back. Tell the students to try to get specific information about where their ancestors were born and how they came to this country. Ask them to bring the information to class and give them an opportunity to share it with the rest of the class. Group youngsters of similar backgrounds together and encourage them to set up a display about the country and customs of people that live there to-day. Suggest that the students include photographs of their families celebrating holidays and other important events in their lives, in the same tradition as their ancestors. Perhaps even set aside a time for the youngsters to invite relatives and friends who could personally share more information about their rich cultural heritage.

SUPPLIES:

Books, magazines, maps to enrich the youngsters' displays.

Mary Frances Cunningham (1859-1940)*

"If you become familiar with our Lord's words and actions, you will have the ever-old, ever-new bible stories in your soul's keeping."
— Mother Demetrias

When she pulled herself up to her full height, Mary Frances Cunningham measured a total of four feet, eleven inches. Enormous energy masked her recurring bouts with poor health. She had clear grey eyes that saw no reason why religious education shouldn't be available to all people, young and not-so-young, regardless of color.

When she noted that her own parish—typical of many, many churches throughout this country in 1884—had Sunday School for white youngsters who attended public schools but quietly ignored the black students, she immediately took steps to correct the situation. Visiting the pastor, she was adamant that there should be "no distinction of color."

"The white children and the black children are the same in God's eyes," she reminded him.

When the pastor explained that Saint Martin's had tried and failed—not once, but four times—she had another solution: give her a place and she'd teach the youngsters herself! And, that's exactly what she did. Not satisfied with only the children who appeared every Sunday morning, she began home visits with the hope of searching out even more who should be attending.

Mary didn't realize at the time that what she was starting on that Sunday morning was the beginning of a work to which she would devote her entire life. She saw nothing extraordinary in what she was about to do; to her way of thinking she was simply doing what needed to be done. Her actions were the natural outgrowth of her own beliefs.

Mary was born in Washington, D.C. When she was ten, her family

---

*EDITOR'S NOTE: This section presents the biographies of three Catholic American women—Mary Frances Cunningham, Rose Hawthorne Lathrop, and Katharine Drexel—with one set of Learning Experiences. All three were born on the East Coast of the United States between 1850-1860, the same decade in which Frances Xavier Cabrini was born in Italy, and they each founded a religious community dedicated to a specific and particular kind of service. In 1900, Rose Hawthorne Lathrop began the Servants of Relief for Incurable Cancer; in 1891, Katharine Drexel started the Blessed Sacrament Sisters for Indians and Colored People; and in May of that same year, Mary Frances Cunningham formed the Mission Helpers of the Sacred Heart. Today many sisters in each of these orders continue the work first begun by one special person.

moved to Baltimore, Maryland, where she attended Saint Peter's Parochial School. In 1870 she made her First Communion and was confirmed the following year. When she finished school, Mary worked as a bookkeeper.

Many who knew her wondered why she did not join a religious order, for she was recognized as a fine teacher. Her love for others and her generous service to them could easily have been channeled into full-time teaching or nursing. The depth of her spiritual life caused her to wonder to herself whether she should become a Carmelite. At that time those were the choices open to a woman who wanted to become a religious—becoming a teacher, a nurse or a contemplative. Though Mary felt that her fulfillment would come through the religious life, she also felt very strongly that her life's work was to be in another field, a field that was not yet open to sisters.

As it turned out, this diminutive woman who shared the same hardy spirit of the pioneers would be the first person to organize a religious order dedicated solely to the work of religious education.

It didn't happen easily. An ordinary event was to be a key point in her life. One morning one of her Sunday School students came to tell her good-bye; the girl's family was moving to another part of Baltimore and would be in a different parish.

"I'm sure they have a Sunday School over there," Mary said. "I'll look into it and let you know."

What Mary found was that there was not only a Sunday School at Saint Peter Claver's, but also a Saint Joseph's Guild which helped the Josephite Fathers by teaching sewing and other useful occupations to the young women of the parish. She immediately joined the Guild's teaching staff, bringing its number to four.

From time to time the four women talked of obtaining more members for the Guild work, and then decided to make a closed retreat together to determine whether or not God's will was the formation of a religious congregation. With the advice of their retreat master, they came to the conclusion that Saint Joseph's Guild should be the nucleus of a religious community which would devote itself to seeking out God's neglected children, teaching them and leading them to become persons of faith. One of the women had no personal desire to be part of this venture and withdrew from the group. Not too long after, another of the women withdrew and entered another congregation, leaving Mary and Mrs. Hartwell, a widow, to develop the initial spark.

Mary's pastor, her spiritual advisor, was hesitant. He felt that the risks were too great, and for about a year he withheld his permission. Finally, after consulting James Cardinal Gibbons about the project, he relented.

Eventually, on May 17, 1891, Mary Frances Cunningham and Mrs. Hartwell pioneered the Mission Helpers of the Sacred Heart. Mary took the name of Sister Demetrias and is credited as being the foundress because she was the only one of the original group to persevere in the work. Mary was finally able to devote her whole life to the work she had done at Saint Martin's in her spare time.

Under her direction these sisters were pioneers in spreading the good news by setting up schools of religion, home instruction programs, with special programs for the handicapped, prisoners and those in hospitals. They were then and continue to be today very visible signs of faith to the communities in which they work and live. Initially the sisters were chartered to work only with blacks, but in 1895, at the urging of a local pastor, Cardinal Gibbons lifted the restriction as to what race they could serve.

Sister Demetrias also pioneered methods of teaching religion. She believed that teaching religion was an art and that it had to be practiced diligently. She insisted that the Mission Helpers be thoroughly prepared for each lesson as she was convinced that every lesson not only should be but could be adapted to suit the age and abilities and interests of each particular class. She was always developing new ways to help the students put the message of the gospel into action in their daily lives. She had created her own method at home when teaching her twelve brothers and sisters and then used it at Saint Martin's where the questions and answers of the Baltimore Catechism were the basic text. Each lesson would begin with a story. Then, when the doctrinal part of the lesson was explained, she would ask the students to show how parts of the story related to the doctrine. Class participation was considered a very necessary and practical method of teaching God's message. Sister Demetrias believed in her work so much that she and the others who joined her never complained of traveling even a whole day in order to teach for an hour and then begin the long return trip home.

Mary Cunningham became Mother Demetrias when she was elected the first Mother General of the Mission Helpers. On the first ballot all the votes were for her, except one—her own. Until she died in 1940 Mother Demetrias remained vitally interested in each of the sisters and actively concerned with their work.

From the beginning there have been many more calls for help than there were sisters to meet the needs. The Mission Helpers are primarily catechists, though they now serve in many capacities from diocesan directors of religious education to census-takers for specific parishes. At present members of the community are stationed in the United States as far west as Arizona and as far south as Puerto Rico.

Nine years after Mother Demetrias died, Rome recognized the Mission Helpers as a religious community and confirmed the mission of this Apostle of Religious Education.

Recommended Readings

Murrett, John C. *The Mary of Saint Martin's.* Westminster, Maryland: Newman, 1960.

Rose Hawthorne Lathrop (1851-1926)

"Human beings owe a debt of love to one another."
— Nathaniel Hawthorne

When the Civil War began in 1861, 10-year-old Rose Hawthorne's family had just returned to Concord, Massachusetts, after having lived in England for seven years and in Spain for two.

On her 13th birthday her father, the prominent author Nathaniel Hawthorne, died. He had been her main tutor, and Rose thought there was no one else quite like him. As a youngster, she had had the chance to know many of his literary friends—Longfellow, Holmes, Whittier, Emerson, Channing and Alcott.

When she was 20, she married George Parsons Lathrop. Their only child, Francis, born in 1876, died of diphtheria only five years later. In 1891, she and her husband were received into the Catholic Church and in 1894 they wrote *A Story of Courage,* a history of the Georgetown Sisters of the Visitation.

That same year, Rose determined that their stormy marriage should be resolved in a permanent separation and, with permission granted from the Bishop of Hartford, she left to go home to Concord to work on a book about her father. Apparently, she did not meet her husband again until he was dying in April, 1898.

As a result of the separation she found she was not prepared to support herself in any particular way; yet this very fact was what led her to discover her special calling. After hearing about the sad plight of a penniless woman who had cancer, Rose decided to devote her life to serving people who found themselves in a similar situation—suffering from inoperable cancer with no money and no place to go.

137

To prepare herself she trained for three months at the New York Cancer Hospital as an unpaid assistant to the nurses; then she began her work on the lower East Side of the city. She sold some of her jewelry, got a check from a friend and rented three small rooms. She bought a few basic medical supplies and bandages and it was not long before her first patient appeared. For financial assistance Rose depended on donations from persons who read her articles about her plans.

On May 1, 1899, these donations made it possible for her to buy a house on Cherry Street in New York City; she named it St. Rose's Free Home. Several women had begun to help her and though most of them left, finding the life too hard and the work too depressing, one stayed with Rose the rest of her life and continued the work after Rose's death.

On December 8, 1900, Mrs. Lathrop chose the name of Sister M. Alphonsa and her faithful associate, Alice Huber, became Sister M. Rose as they took their first vows and were given the white habit and black veil of the Dominican Sisters. This officially established the Dominican Congregation of St. Rose of Lima and the women called themselves the Servants of Relief for Incurable Cancer.

As the community grew, its work expanded. Soon they were looking for larger quarters and there was the ever-present need for more revenue. The motherhouse, its novitiate and a cancer home were established at what was once a large summer hotel north of White Plains in Westchester County and aid for the patients was secured through Mother Alphonsa's magazine,

Christ's Poor, and through her series of published reports.

When she was 75 years old, she was the chosen recipient of the annual medal given by the Rotary Club of New York for her outstanding work. The message engraved on it said: "In recognition of her Mercy and Valor and the free gift of a life of service to destitute sufferers." A few evenings later (July 19, 1926), Mother Alphonsa died in her sleep.

The work she began continues today. Her sisters provide gentle care for indigent cancer patients in New York and at other homes elsewhere in the United States.

Recommended Readings

Myers, Rawley. *People Who Loved.* Notre Dame: Fides, 1970.

Burton, Katherine Kurz. *In No Strange Land.* New York: Longmans, Green & Co., 1942.

Katharine Drexel (1858-1955)

"Before you die, be good to your friends and give them a share in what you possess."

— Sirach 14:13

During the 19th century very few religious congregations served the Negro in America. There were the Josephite Fathers and the Society of the Divine Word, pledged to work in black parishes, and there were all-Negro communities of sisters such as the Oblate Sisters of Providence (see biography of Elizabeth Lange), the Handmaids of Mary and the Sisters of the Holy Family. A third group, the Sisters of the Blessed Sacrament, was founded by Mother Katharine Drexel and they dedicated themselves to work among Negroes and Native Americans.

Katharine Drexel, part of the wealthy Philadelphia banking family, was born in that city on November 26, 1858. Her mother died while Katharine was an infant and her father remarried two years later. She had a happy family life, at first receiving her education at home with private governesses and later traveling in Europe.

In 1884, when she was 26, the Third Plenary Council of Baltimore (presided over by Archbishop Gibbons) legislated for missionary activity among native Americans and Negroes. Katharine inherited a fortune with the deaths of her stepmother (1883) and her father (1885) and wanted to donate it to further this particular apostolate. During a visit to Rome she told Leo XIII of her plan and asked him to recommend a particular religious order that would use the money only for the Indians and Negroes. In response, the Pope invited her to be their missionary herself!

She accepted the challenge and in 1889 she began her novitiate with the Sisters of Mercy of Pittsburgh, Pennsylvania. Two years later she and a few companions began the Sisters of the Blessed Sacrament for Indians and Colored People in a convent made over from the Drexel family summer home in Torresdale, Pennsylvania.

Many requests for help soon came from Southern Negro centers and from Indian missions in the Southwest. In response, Mother Katharine built and maintained missions and staffed them with sisters. Schools and convents in Columbus (Ohio), Chicago, Boston and Harlem soon followed. In 1915 she and several of her sisters established Xavier University in New Orleans, Louisiana, the only Catholic university in the Western Hemisphere with a predominantly Negro student body.

In 1935 Mother Drexel suffered a heart attack; she was now 77, but even so, she was able to continue her work for 20 years more. An invalid during her last years, she spent most of her day in prayer. At the time of her death in 1955, she had used more than $12 million of her inheritance for the Negroes and the Native Americans of the United States.

Recommended Readings
>Burton, Katherine Kurz. *The Golden Door*. New York: P. J. Kenedy & Sons, 1957.

Learning Experience
Primary Level

TEACHER NOTES:
Before telling the children about the women covered in this chapter, ask the class to locate pictures in magazines of people helping one another and to bring one of the pictures to school.

The rest of this experience will involve a long-range project lasting several weeks. Have two fairly large containers available. Fill one with two-inch squares of red, orange, yellow, green, blue, indigo and violet construction paper (for constructing a "rainbow" on the wall). You may want to cut out letters and put a poem on the wall such as:

>Think of others.
>Let it show!
>Build our rainbow. Watch it grow!

(The actual responsibility for putting up the parts of the rainbow will be yours because it will involve standing on a chair in order to reach the high parts.)

LEARNING EXPERIENCE: "Rainbow" Project
After telling the stories about these three women to the children, talk with them about how these women each saw a special job that needed to

be done and then did it! Suggest to the class that every day each of us has many opportunities to do kind things for others. Talk about the magazine pictures the children brought from home.

You may want to say something like the following: "Sometimes it is hard, but everytime we do a kind deed, we are helping the world to be a better place, a happier place. As a sign that we are helping others every day, we are going to build a rainbow on this wall. Every time you do something to help another, you may take a colored square, write a couple of words on it describing what you did and put the square in the other container. You may choose whatever color you prefer. I will put the squares on the wall after I put some tape on the back of them."

SUPPLIES:

Two-inch squares of colored paper, tape, containers, pencils, a fairly large blank wall.

Learning Experience
Intermediate Level

TEACHER NOTES:

Prayer is a special part of our lives just as it was in the lives of Rose Hawthorne Lathrop, Katharine Drexel and Mary Frances Cunningham.

Invite the youngsters to create a classroom prayer book called *Silence Speaks.* Allowing a few days for the homework assignment, ask them to collect large, colored pictures from magazines of things that happen without making a sound (e.g., blink of an eye, rose bud opening, spider spinning a web, etc.).

LEARNING EXPERIENCE: Classroom Prayer Book

When sufficient pictures have been brought into the classroom, help the children to develop a short text to accompany each illustration such as, "Wonderful things happen in stillness! Did you ever hear a plant when it pops through the soil?"

Build toward the idea that often God "speaks" to us during very quiet times.

Tape the pictures onto separate pieces of poster board and write the text with magic markers. Have the last page be a suggestion for the readers to tell—through poetry, a paragraph, drawing or photography—about their special places for quiet prayer. Cover each page with clear contact paper and use ribbon or metal fasteners to hold the pages together.

SUPPLIES:

Pictures, poster board, magic markers, clear contact paper.

Learning Experience
Junior High Level

TEACHER NOTES:

Reproduce copies of the following passage from the Old Testament: Proverbs 31:12, 14-16, 18, 20, 25-27, 29-31.

LEARNING EXPERIENCE: Scripture Passage

After presenting and discussing any questions about the biographies of these three women, distribute copies of the Old Testament passage to the youngsters in your class. Invite them to read it thoughtfully and to question: How does this apply to the women we just studied?

Ask the class to jot down their ideas so nothing will be lost or overlooked during the discussion to follow. Then have volunteers share their thoughts.

SUPPLIES:

Copies of Old Testament passage, paper, pencils or pens.

Paraliturgical Celebration for Unit IV
Toward a New Social Awareness

Theme:

Each one of the women: Frances Xavier Cabrini, Mary Frances Cunningham, Rose Hawthorne Lathrop and Katharine Drexel, whose lives we have explored in this Unit, grew up in an era when women generally assumed the role of bearing children and devoting their lives to the welfare of their families. Because of their faith, each chose to leave behind the security of these established traditions, as well as material and monetary wealth. They dedicated themselves instead to the educational, spiritual, and physical welfare of the wider family of man. Let us celebrate today the creative expression of their faith and the way they inspired others to follow in their footsteps.

Entrance Hymn:

"I Heard the Lord," Jacob Krieger, *Songs of Praise,* The Word of God Music; "Enter, O People of God," *People's Mass Book,* W.L.P.

Penitential Rite:

For the times I have failed to help someone in need because I would not give up cherished time, privileges or even money, Lord, have mercy.

LORD, HAVE MERCY.

For the times I failed to help someone because I was afraid that my friends might not share my concern and think that I was "different," Christ, have mercy.

CHRIST, HAVE MERCY.

For the times I have not trusted that you would give me the strength to follow your unselfish example and the courage to lead others to service in your name, Lord, have mercy.

LORD, HAVE MERCY.

145

First Reading:
(Colossians 3:12-17)

Gospel Reading:
(Mark 10:17-23, 26-31)

Homily:
Through your remarks help the youngsters to understand that, when these four women made their decisions to serve the poor, the sick and the disadvantaged, they made many great sacrifices. They had no assurances that they would be accepted by those they chose to serve or that they would be successful at serving them. The way they faced the uncertainty of their new lives reflected their complete trust in God and encouraged many others to join them.

Song:
"If You Bring Your Gift to the Altar," Lucien Deiss, *People's Mass Book,* W.L.P.; "Lord, Make Us Ready," Tom Parker, *People's Mass Book,* W.L.P.; "Of My Hands," Ray Repp, *Hymnal for Young Christians,* F.E.L.; "Love Round," *Songs of Praise,* The Word of God Music; "Come Before the Table of the Lord," Tom Parker, *People's Mass Book,* W.L.P.; "Follow Christ," Sebastian Temple, Franciscan Communications Center.

Meditation:
An interpretive dance and dramatic reading of the poem, "An Outstretched Hand" by Rod McKuen.*

> Each of us was made by God
> and some of us grew tall.
> Others stood in the wind
> their branches bent and fell.
> Those of us who walk in light
> must help the ones in darkness up.
> For that's what life is all about
> and love is all there is to life.

> Each of us was made by God
> beautiful in his mind's eye.
> Those of us that turned out sound
> should look across our shoulders once
> and help the weak ones to their feet.

> It only takes an outstretched hand.

* "An Outstretched Hand," Rod McKuen, from *Lonesome Cities,* Random House, New York, New York. With permission.

Note:

Sometime before the liturgy, discuss with one youngster or a small group of youngsters the words and meaning of Rod McKuen's poem as it relates to this celebration of the lives of these four great American Catholic women. Encourage them to reflect on the poem and to express what it means to them through a series of simple, connected body movements. Assist the youngster or youngsters in creating a short and simple interpretive dance to be presented either during or after a dramatic reading of the poem, "The Outstretched Hand," with very soft music either recorded, taped, or played live in the background.

Recessional:

"Follow Me," John Denver, *John Denver's Greatest Hits,* RCA CPL 1-0374 Stereo, "Come, Follow Me," Ann Caldwallader, *Songs of Praise,* The Word of God Music, "I Have Decided to Follow Jesus," traditional, *Songs of Praise,* The Word of God Music.

UNIT V

Reshaping the Nation and the World

Alfred E. Smith (1873-1943)

"We have been slow to legislate along the direction that means thanksgiving to the poorest man recorded in history—to Him who was born in a stable in Bethlehem."

— Al Smith

Three years before the nation celebrated its centennial anniversary, Al Smith was born in New York City's lower East Side on December 30. The Civil War had been over for eight years and Ulysses S. Grant was President. The nation was attracting huge numbers of immigrants and was in the midst of changing from a rural country to one of urban communities. It was also faced with one of the longest economic depressions in American history beginning in 1873 and dragging on into the 1880's.

At this time the cities were finding places for the many immigrants arriving from Europe. The majority were Catholics and the only people who seemed interested in helping these new arrivals—besides their parish priests—were the bosses of the cities' political machines. These usually corrupt organizations provided them with many badly needed services. A local machine had the power to find jobs for faithful supporters, to take care of hospital bills, or arrange for necessary legal help. To very poor families it might donate turkey baskets for holidays and supplies of coal during the winter. Sometimes local politicians sponsored boat rides or outings in the park as a welcome relief from the summer's heat for young people and older ones alike. In return, the recipients were expected to remain loyal to their benefactors' party, close their eyes to graft and corruption and, above all, vote in every election according to instructions.

Best known was Tammany Hall, an organization founded in 1789, which then controlled New York City. Like other organizations it held its power by winning votes through the favors it could distribute. Its worst phase was under "Boss" William Marcy Tweed. After his downfall (1871),

151

Tammany experienced a series of purges—increasingly thoroughgoing. The greatest force in this reformation process was Alfred E. Smith, who, though he was never head of Tammany, began as a district leader before rising to a higher office.

When he was 30 he was elected to the New York State Assembly for the first time. Though thoroughly loyal to the Democratic party and well-known for his honesty, he distinguished himself in Albany by the careful and independent thought he gave to issues and problems. He studied and mastered state government and in 10 years he served as the Speaker of the Assembly (1913). (In the meantime, he had also been elected sheriff of New York City.) In 1917, he obtained a position on the Port Authority where his efficient work led him to the governorship of New York State the next year.

For four terms he served as governor in an extraordinary manner; his was a sound business administration, free of favoritism in appointments. He consistently battled for the underdog and was a pioneer in calling for social improvement by government.

His own life combined with his religious convictions made him a champion of the poor. He had known what it was like to live in a crowded tenement; this personal experience may have helped him develop sympathy for people who had to live in the slums. He had learned to swim in the East River, already being polluted by factory and human wastes; this may have helped him see early some of the problems of an industrial nation. As positive contributions, he pushed through social welfare laws that bene-fited the poor, widows, children and working people.

He conserved the scenic resources of the state by acquiring parks and beaches; he built the first good network of roads so the working people could travel to these parks. He made more money available for education; he improved factory working conditions and initiated housing developments. Because he was in touch with the people's problems, they often called him the "common man."

In the 1920's, cities were influencing American life and the problems of their people were beginning to come to the surface. The presidential election in 1928 seemed to show that Americans felt strongly about the increasing importance of their cities. Nominated by the Democrats, Al Smith was only the second presidential candidate of a major party to come from a large city.

They could hardly have chosen a man better suited to represent the vast majority of the big city immigrants. He, like them, had had a limited education; he had begun work at 14 after finishing St. James Parochial School; and he was a devout Catholic as were most of the immigrants. He was also against prohibition.

Now the country came face-to-face with the religious issue. In the White House there had been nine Episcopalians, five Presbyterians, four Unitarians, four Methodists, two Dutch Reformed and one each of the Disciples of Christ, Congregationalist and Baptist faiths, but no Catholic. Anti-Catholic prejudice appeared on the scene.

Various rumors and many charges against Smith were circulated. One was a picture captioned with the message that Al Smith had opened "a secret underground tunnel to the Vatican." In actuality he was cutting the ribbon inaugurating service on the Eighth Avenue subway. Throughout the campaign Smith attempted to dispose of the religious question by trying to convince his attackers that there was no conflict between Americanism and Catholicism. Despite these attacks made on him because of his religion, he never tried to play it down. His faith was genuine and open, and he was proud of it. For many years he was an altar server at St. James; he accepted positions on Catholic committees, was seen frequently with members of the hierarchy and let it be known that he was a good friend of the Archbishop of New York City, Patrick Joseph Cardinal Hayes.

In truth, an equally basic issue in the election was that of prohibition. The country may not yet have been ready to accept a Catholic President, but it was even less ready to accept the return of legal liquor. (Prohibition was repealed five years later in 1933.)

After failing to win the presidential nomination in 1932 from his party (the Democrats chose Franklin Delano Roosevelt), Al Smith, now 59, became president of the corporation that erected the Empire State Building. He took little part in politics after this and devoted himself actively to the management of the Empire State Building. His wife, Katie, whom he married in 1900, died on May 4, 1943, and he died on October 4 of the same year.

In New York State he is remembered as one of its greatest governors, a man of sterling character and a man of progressive social legislation.

Recommended Readings

Handlin, Oscar. *Al Smith and His America.* Boston: Little, Brown, 1958.

Moore, Edmund. *A Catholic Runs for President: The Campaign of 1928.* Gloucester, Maine: Peter Smith, 1956.

O'Connor, Richard. *First Hurrah: A Biography of Alfred E. Smith, Happy Warrior.* New York: Putnam, 1970.

Learning Experience
Primary Level

TEACHER NOTES:

When you have related the biography of Al Smith to the children, review some of the major events in his life by focusing the children's attention on his role as politician and on the many contributions he made to others through his dedicated public service. Ask the children the following questions:

- Would you like to be governor of your state or president of the United States some day? Why?
- What are some of the things you would try to do for others if you were elected governor or president?

LEARNING EXPERIENCE: Buttons and Bumper Stickers

Explain to the children that before people are elected to serve in public office they make many speeches and talk personally to many people all over the country about the good things they hope to do when they are elected. Pass out contact paper strips (about 12" x 3") and round precut pieces of contact paper and ask the children to make bumper stickers and campaign buttons to tell others about the things that Al Smith did as a politician and about the good things they would do if they were politicians. Give them indelible magic markers to decorate their bumper stickers and buttons with words and symbols. Set aside a special time for them to share and wear their creations.

SUPPLIES:

Contact paper, scissors, indelible magic markers.

Learning Experience
Intermediate Level

TEACHER NOTES:

Once you have related the information in the biography of Al Smith to the youngsters, bring them to a deeper appreciation of the responsibilities they as American citizens and possibly elected public officials will have to assume, by involving them in a series of informal debates characteristic of those held at various times in "town meetings" all over our country.

LEARNING EXPERIENCE: Town Meeting

Remind the youngsters that Al Smith, as a politician, had to make many difficult decisions on issues that did not always have easy answers. Mention that, as citizens with the responsibility to vote, they too will have to make important decisions on major issues concerning their fellow Americans. Separate the class in half, appoint two moderators, and pass out to one half of the class index cards on which are clearly stated various important issues. Challenge the youngsters with the index cards to formulate an opinion and take a stand on the issue at the "town meeting." Tell the youngsters in the other half of the class to represent the opposing side of the issue so that all possibilities for its solution can be explored. The moderators should see to it that "equal time" is given to each speaker and that everyone has an opportunity to be heard. Select relevant issues concerning the youngsters' school, Church, community and country as topics for debate and be sure that all comments are respectfully received.

SUPPLIES:

Relevant issues on index cards.

Learning Experience
Junior High Level

TEACHER NOTES:

Share the biography of Al Smith with the students and, after a brief period for questions and discussion, give them a "think piece" to reflect on silently for a few minutes. . .

"Each time a man stands up for an ideal, or acts to improve the lot of others, or strikes out against injustices, he sends forth a tiny ripple of hope, and crossing each other from a million different centers of energy and daring, these ripples build a current that can sweep down the mightiest walls of oppression and resistence." From a speech by Robert Kennedy.

LEARNING EXPERIENCE: "Think Piece"

Explain to the students that the passage they have just considered was written some years ago by a politician named Robert Kennedy. Pass out paper, old magazines and newspapers and invite the students to show through symbols, pictures or words what Robert Kennedy's speech means to them. When the youngsters have finished their work, encourage them to share their thoughts with the other members of the class. Encourage them to discuss how the passage relates to the role of a Christian politician in our world.

SUPPLIES:

Scissors, old magazines and newspapers, magic markers, paste.

Dorothy Day (1897-   )

". . . man is supposed to transform his world so that it bears a mark of his own intelligence and his own concern, because only if that is there can there be a Christian dimension to all this."
— Bernard Cooke

The words of William F. Jabusch's song, "Whatsoever You Do," seem to be especially appropriate when talking about the life and the work of Dorothy Day.

> When I was hungry, you gave me to eat;
> When I was thirsty, you gave me to drink. . .
> When I was homeless, you opened your door;
> When I was naked, you gave me your coat.

These lines beautifully describe some of the ways in which she serves others. For over 40 years she has held "open house" in New York City, offering food, clothing and shelter to those in need. Every day she takes the works of mercy so seriously that they actually form her way of life.

What made her choose this particular life-style? And how did she get started? Born in Brooklyn, New York, in 1897, she was the third of five children. When she was six her family moved to California and lived there until just after the San Francisco earthquake (1906). That terrible disaster and the fires that resulted destroyed a good part of the city and killed hundreds of people.

> What I remember most plainly about the Earthquake was the human warmth and kindliness of everyone afterward. . . . Mother and all our neighbors were busy from morning to night cooking hot meals. They gave away every extra garment they possessed.*

* Dorothy Day, *Meditations*, p. 6. Originally appeared in *From Union Square to Rome* by Dorothy Day.

159

When the family moved, they settled in Chicago. By the time Dorothy was 18 she had finished two years of college at the University of Illinois. She recalls in *The Long Loneliness,* "The ugliness of life in a world which professed itself to be Christian appalled me. . . . I felt my faith had nothing in common with that of Christians around me. . . . So I hardened my heart." Looking for a community which shared her concerns and values she joined the Socialist party.

When she was 19 the family moved to New York City, and Dorothy went to work as a reporter and columnist on the *New York Call,* a socialist daily paper.

Recalling this time in her life while speaking at Bridgewater State College in Massachusetts a few years ago, she said she had been so horrified by the conditions under which she saw the poor living that she decided the only way to get over her aversion was to share their misery. So, she moved out of her parents' home into an unheated, poorly lit New York tenement. "To bathe, I had to walk half a mile to a municipal shower. Some people in New York still have to do that."

For a year she worked for five dollars a week and wrote a column which emphasized the sordidness of slum living. The next year she joined some Columbia University students who were protesting U. S. involvement in World War I, worked briefly for the Anti-Conscription League, then joined the staff of *The Masses.* Though her name became closely associated with the Communist party because of her writings in radical publications, she did not sign up as a member.

She thought about becoming a Catholic for many years before actually converting. In *From Union Square to Rome* she wrote, "You will be surprised but there was many a morning . . . that I went to an early Mass at St. Joseph's Church on Sixth Avenue. It was just around the corner from where I lived, and seeing people going to an early weekday Mass attracted me. What were they finding there? I seemed to feel the faith of those about me and I longed for their faith. . . . I prayed for the gift of faith. I was sure, yet not sure. I postponed the day of decision."

She was baptized a Catholic when she was 30. "It was in December, 1927, a most miserable day, and the trip was long from the city down to Tottenville, Staten Island. . . . A year later my confirmation was indeed joyful and Pentecost never passes without a renewed sense of happiness and thanksgiving."

Dorothy Day continued writing for socialist publications and on December 10, 1932, she met Peter Maurin, a French-born Roman Catholic layman. He had an idea for a "green revolution" that would unite scholars and workers together in houses of hospitality, in farming communes and in round-table discussions.

Peter's idea of hospices seemed a simple and logical one to me, hospices such as they had in the Middle Ages were certainly very much needed today. But I liked even better his talks about personal responsibility. He quoted St. Jerome, that every house should have a "Christ's room" for our brother who was in need. That "the coat which hangs in one's closet belongs to the poor." Living in tenements as I had for years I had found many of the poorest practicing these teachings . . . Peter brought up the idea of a paper the first time I met him and he kept harping on it, day after day. He told me I needed a Catholic background, and he came day after day with books and papers and digests of articles which he either read aloud or left with me to read.

It was impossible to be with a person like Peter without sharing his simple faith that the Lord would provide what was necessary to do His work.*

The first issue of the paper, titled *The Catholic Worker*, was distributed on May Day, 1933. It declared that it would "popularize and make known the encyclicals of the popes in regard to social justice." It also addressed many problems, from labor issues to race relations, and the staff soon had to find ways to house and feed the unemployed who began knocking at the paper's office door. In response, Saint Joseph's House of Hospitality was born, the first of 33 sanctuaries they would found throughout the country for the poor.

Today, the name, Dorothy Day, brings many images to mind: long bread lines . . . penny newspapers . . . hospitality houses . . . soup kitchens . . . Catholic Worker. The last term actually refers to two separate but closely related things, a monthly newspaper and the social movement she founded with her friend, Peter Maurin.

Though some people think Dorothy Day qualifies as a modern saint, all agree that she has and does make us aware of our responsibility to care for others by doing so herself. Her first attempts were solely through newspaper columns; then she thought the Socialist party held promise. Finally, as a convert to Catholicism and after meeting Peter Maurin she combined her journalism talents with the ideas they shared and together they formed the basis of the Catholic Worker Movement.

This movement held a strong appeal for those who were not content simply to talk or read about social reform. Young men and women left their jobs and went to the Catholic Worker to work for nothing except their room and board and clothes. They marched on picket lines, ran soup

* Dorothy Day, *Meditations*, pp. 12-13. Originally appeared in *House of Hospitality* by Dorothy Day.

kitchens and went out to the country to prove, usually unsuccessfully, that men could find work, food and shelter on the land.

Dorothy Day continues to live today in voluntary poverty and to speak out for the right of every individual to be free from hunger and to be free from unnecessary suffering. Today there are varying numbers of houses of hospitality throughout the country, autonomous, yet keeping in touch with each other through the pages of *The Catholic Worker*. Usually eight pages in length, it has a circulation of 85,000. "For office equipment we have a stencil machine held together with hairpins, and three typewriters. Everyone helps put out the paper, men from the bread line, staff members, visitors." Dorothy Day still writes for it, contributing her "On Pilgrimage" column to it every month.

In New York there is both a hospitality house and a farm in Tivoli where the homeless can still find food, clothing and shelter. Dorothy Day continues to serve as an inspiration through her articles, her books, lectures, her radio and television appearances, and particularly through her way of life. The witness of this five-foot, nine-inch woman with lively blue eyes is a compelling example of love for the least of Christ's brothers and sisters.

Recommended Readings

Day, Dorothy. *Meditations.* (Stanley Vishnewski, ed.) New York: Newman, 1970.

Miller, William D. *A Harsh and Dreadful Love: Dorothy Day and the Catholic Worker.* New York: Liveright, 1973.

Learning Experience
Primary Level

TEACHER NOTES:

After you have related the information from the biography of Dorothy Day to the children, talk with them about the many kind things she did in her lifetime for others. Focus their attention on the "soup kitchen" she began in New York City and guide them in a discussion of the people it served, why it was necessary and how it and many others like it operate in cities and towns all over the United States today.

LEARNING EXPERIENCE: Place Mats

Supply the children with construction paper and magic markers and invite them to make "place mats" to remind them of Dorothy Day's many good works . . . including the "soup kitchen" she started for the poor in New York City. Have the children draw pictures on the construction paper, perhaps of the "soup kitchen" or any other major event in her life, and then cut two pieces of wax paper about an inch larger than the youngsters' drawings to cover their "place mats" on both sides. Using a warm iron, gently press the pieces of wax paper over their construction paper drawings, being sure to seal the edges. If you have sufficient time and resources, encourage the children to make place mats about Dorothy Day for each member of their family.

SUPPLIES:
Construction paper, magic markers, wax paper and warm iron. *Caution:* Primary Level children are not capable of working with an electric iron.

Learning Experience
Intermediate Level

TEACHER NOTES:
When the youngsters have had time to reflect on the information in the biography about Dorothy Day, draw them into a discussion of her life and work by asking a few pertinent questions:
* What experiences in Dorothy Day's life influenced her decision to help the poor and hungry in New York City?
* What were some of the things she did to help people without food or a place to stay?
* Why do you think she felt it was so important to write about the problems of the poor in her newspaper, *The Catholic Worker?*

LEARNING EXPERIENCE: Advertising Campaign for Charitable Organizations
Before class make a list of several charitable organizations in your community or diocese which distribute food to poor families. Tell the youngsters about the organizations when they come to class and invite them to support an organization's good work by bringing it to the attention of their families, friends and fellow parishioners through an "advertising campaign." Encourage the youngsters to make posters and prepare flyers to make people more aware of the existence of each organization, its needs and the people it helps. Remind them to include accurate information about what, where and how people can contribute either their time, food, clothing or money to help the poor in their area. Provide the youngsters with large poster paper, paint, magic markers and crayons and designate specific places where their posters should be hung. Suggest that they ask their parents for food contributions and even perhaps contribute some of their own allowance so that the class as a whole may make a small donation to one or all of the organizations.

SUPPLIES:
Poster paper, crayons.

Learning Experience
Junior High Level

TEACHER NOTES:

When the students have had time to explore the biography of Dorothy Day, involve them in a discussion centering around the particular life-style she has chosen and why. Suggest that her life-style makes a unique statement about her beliefs and encourage the youngsters to react to those beliefs.

LEARNING EXPERIENCE: "Moments With" Dorothy Day

Separate the class into groups of four or five and challenge each group to select approximately ten slides from an available series and an accompanying musical recording which they believe best relates Dorothy Day's special care and concern for her fellowman. When each group has decided on their slides and music provide them with a schedule of dates and times when they can share their impressions and a few "moments with" this great Catholic American.

SUPPLIES:

Slide series and musical recordings focusing on themes of sharing, suffering, poverty, people, etc., slide projector, record player or cassette player.

Thomas A. Dooley (1927-1961)

"Give us thy worthy children,
The blessings of wisdom and speech,
And the hands and the hearts of healing,
And the lips and the tongues to teach."
— Thomas A. Dooley

Born in 1927 in St. Louis, Missouri, Thomas Dooley was one of four boys in a well-to-do Catholic family. He had a carefree childhood, and enjoyed all the comforts of life, including a fine education. He attended the University of Notre Dame and eventually graduated from St. Louis University Medical School as a doctor. In 1953, because of his strong sense of duty to his country (and influenced by his brother Earle's death in World War II), Tom Dooley accepted a commission in the U.S. Navy.

From that time on his life was to contain few carefree moments. A growing awareness of the tremendous importance of each irreplaceable hour was to cause him to restructure his life so that he lived every hour as though the lives of thousands depended on it.

Tom Dooley remembered Walt Whitman's line, "It's not so important what you do with the years of your life, but it's very important what you do with each hour." His life offers convincing evidence that he was committed to the truth of that statement.

When the Northern Viet Minh first moved south to conquer the Vietnamese nation, the people caught in the midst of the conflict felt the effects of Tom Dooley's concern. Assigned to temporary duty on the *U.S.S. Montague,* he and a small crew were given the task of transporting the northern refugees to safety in the southern city of Saigon.

As the only medical doctor aboard ship, Tom Dooley was responsible for treating hundreds of refugees suffering from malnutrition, disease and mutilation by Communist torture. Three months later he was transferred to duty as an interpreter and medical officer in the port city of Haiphong.

167

With the help of a small medical staff there, he built camps, requisitioned supplies and cared for nearly 600,000 displaced persons.

Tom Dooley wrote of his experiences, "We had seen simple tender loving care change a people's fear and hatred into friendship and understanding. We had witnessed the power of medical aid . . . to reach the hearts and souls of a nation." As the sights and sounds of human suffering awakened him to the desperate needs of the people in Asia, the lines of a poem by Robert Frost seemed to echo in his mind:

> The woods are lovely, dark and deep,
> But I have promises to keep,
> And miles to go before I sleep,
> And miles to go before I sleep.

In the years that followed, those lines became an expression of his commitment to relieve that suffering with the skill and knowledge of medicine and with Christian love!

In his first book, *Deliver Us from Evil,* Tom Dooley passionately documented his own role in the Navy's successful peacetime operation in Southeast Asia. For his heroic role in that operation the Navy awarded him the Legion of Merit and the government of Vietnam awarded him its highest honor. The events chronicled in his first book were, however, only a prelude to the drama yet to unfold in his life. The atrocities he had seen in his 11 months of service had been for him a revelation from which he envisioned possibilities "for transferring the brotherhood of man from an ideal into a reality that people could understand." When he resigned from the Navy in 1956 he vowed to return to Southeast Asia to help "those miserable and diseased people who, in the depths of anguish, have hearts so splendid and faith so powerful."

Tom Dooley chose Laos as his first "missionary field" and devised a realistic plan to set up mobile medical units in the jungles to treat people in surrounding areas. He lost no time in gathering men and resources to implement it.

With sales of his first book as the primary source of funds, Dooley purchased some basic medical equipment and financed its transportation to Laos. Generous donations, including a projector and films from Walt Disney and valuable supplies from large pharmaceutical companies provided the other essential items needed. After personally seeking approval for his venture from the U.S. State Department and the Laotian ambassador, Tom Dooley arrived in Laos determined to bind up the wounds of the suffering people there.

Within a few months after his arrival his idea of "people to people, heart to heart" contact began to take hold and he had started to train local natives who he hoped would eventually staff and continue to run the paramedical units. Eager to share his adventure and to inspire others to join in it, Tom Dooley began writing his second book, *Edge of Tomorrow.* In it he related a prayer that was a continual source of inspiration to him and his fellow workers that first year,

>   Give us, thy worthy children,
>   The blessings of wisdom and speech,
>   And the hands and the hearts of healing,
>   And the lips and the tongues to teach.

In the next few years his books received wide acclaim; He and all the people associated with his project drew national attention. Supplies, financial donations, volunteers, prayers and encouragement poured into Tom Dooley's stateside office offering needed support for his programs. He welcomed the generous support and responded enthusiastically to it by seeking the sponsorship of the already well-established International Rescue Committee for his medical operation. They agreed to take his organization under their wing by adopting it as the Medical International Cooperation or Medico. Tom Dooley asked Dr. Albert Schweitzer, whom he had long admired, to be its patron. Dr. Schweitzer accepted the request and wrote Dooley, "I do not know what your destiny will ever be, but this I do know . . . You will always have happiness if you seek and find: how to serve."

In his third book, *The Night They Burned the Mountain,* Tom Dooley wrote about his experiences in the field and recorded the tragedy of his own unfortunate illness as well. Removal of a malignant tumor from his chest in 1959 uncovered a fast-spreading cancer; the book was to become the diary of this dying man.

Major surgery to remove the tissue affected by the cancer was performed in New York City in August, 1959. CBS television requested permission to do a documentary of the operation in the interests of medicine and education and Tom Dooley consented. After the surgery, he reflected on the mission still ahead of him, "The cancer went no deeper than my flesh; there was no cancer in my spirit. . . . I would keep my appetite for a high quality of life. In whatever time was left, I would continue to help the clots and clusters of the withered and wretched in Asia to the utmost of my ability. Maybe I could now be tender in a better way. I was a member of the fellowship of those who bear the mark of pain."

For one more year Dr. Dooley served his fellowman well. On Jan. 25, 1961, he died. In 1962, President Kennedy honored him posthumously with the Congressional Medal inscribed, "In recognition of the Public Service to alleviate suffering among people of the world." The trend of humanitarian service he began with Medico continues today in association with CARE, Inc., as a tribute to this great man.

Recommended Readings

Dooley, Thomas A. *Doctor Tom Dooley: My Story.* New York: Farrar, Straus, Giroux, 1962.

Dooley, Thomas A. *Doctor Tom Dooley's Three Great Books: Deliver Us from Evil, The Edge of Tomorrow* and *The Night They Burned the Mountain.* New York: Farrar, Straus, Giroux, 1960.

Elliott, Lawrence. *The Legacy of Tom Dooley.* Cleveland: World, 1969.

Monahan, James. *Before I Sleep: Last Days of Thomas Dooley.* New York: Farrar, Straus, Giroux, 1961.

Myers, Rawley. *People Who Loved.* Notre Dame: Fides, 1970.

Learning Experience
Primary Level

TEACHER NOTES:

After you have related the story of Tom Dooley to the children, talk with them about the many ways he, like Jesus, helped his fellowman. Refer to scriptural passages the children are familiar with where Jesus healed the sick or fed the hungry, and point out to the children that Tom Dooley, in his lifetime, tried to do the same.

LEARNING EXPERIENCE: Drawings and Song

Pass out construction paper and crayons or magic markers and ask the children to make a picture showing how Tom Dooley, like Jesus, was a good friend to others. When the children finish their drawings mount them and hang them in a special place in the room. Give each child an opportunity to comment on his drawing and then teach the whole class the song, "How Can I Be a Friend?" by Lou Fortunate.

SUPPLIES:
Construction paper, crayons or magic markers.

Learning Experience
Intermediate Level

TEACHER NOTES:
After the youngsters have had time to reflect on the biography of Tom Dooley, gather them together for a short discussion of his life and work. Point out to the youngsters that the idea of helping others to help themselves was central to the operation of Tom Dooley's organization and then offer them an opportunity to make a similar contribution.

LEARNING EXPERIENCE: "Walk-a-thon," "Bike-a-thon"
Suggest that the youngsters in the class plan and participate in a "walk-a-thon" or "bike-a-thon" to raise money for the organization which Tom Dooley founded (Medico, which merged with CARE, Inc., in 1962) or for any other organization dedicated to the same type of work. Have the youngsters make up a "sponsor sheet" to explain the purpose of their class project and to indicate where any funds collected would be sent. Leave a space at the bottom of the sheet for contributors to designate how much money they will give to support the project for every mile a youngster walks or bikes with classmates on a specified day. Type the "sponsor sheet" and have enough copies of it made so that the youngsters in the class can be given one sheet for every sponsor they can find in their parish or neighborhood to support the project. Set aside a day for the bike- or walk-a-thon (and an alternate day in case of rain), find a suitable route for the youngsters to travel and enlist parents to serve at check points where the "miles" the youngsters traveled can be tallied and marked on their sponsor sheets. After the bike-a-thon tell the youngsters to bring their validated sheets to the sponsors and collect their contributions. Plan a celebration for the day the youngsters bring in contributions and congratulate them on a job well done. End the celebration with a reading of the lines from Robert Frost's poem,

> The woods are lovely, dark and deep,
> But I have promises to keep,
> And miles to go before I sleep,
> And miles to go before I sleep.

SUPPLIES:
Paper, stencil or ditto for copying "sponsor sheets."

Learning Experience
Junior High Level

TEACHER NOTES:
    Once the students have explored the biography of Tom Dooley, and have become familiar with the main events in his life, challenge them to write a folk song with lyrics celebrating his great contributions to people all over the world.

LEARNING EXPERIENCE: Folk Song
    Suggest that the students write the lyrics to the tune of some popular American folk song such as "Yankee Doodle" or "Clementine" and that the lyrics relate the life of Tom Dooley in narrative form. Have on hand for their inspiration and reference several copies of Tom Dooley's books and arrange a date and time for them to sing their folk song for classmates, family or friends. In the formal presentation of their work before an audience they may wish to read short passages of Tom Dooley's books in between stanzas of the song they created.

SUPPLIES:
    Tom Dooley's books (optional).

Cesar Chavez (1927-   )

"The truest act of courage, the strongest act of manliness, is to sacrifice ourselves for others in a totally nonviolent struggle for justice."

— Cesar Chavez

A blowup of this poem covers the wall in the office of the United Farm Workers at Salinas, California:

> My Father . . .
> could never write a poem.
> But when he lined up his plow,
> with a pine tree on a distant hill,
> he made a furrow,
> straight as an arrow,
> across the length of his labor.
>
> My Father . . .
> could not write very many words.
> But when he brought in
> his crop
> in the heat of a summer afternoon,
> he created
> a poem . . . from the earth.

Although this very simple and beautiful poem was intended to describe a Mexican farmworker, it might just as well have described the labors of thousands of Americans who came to this country with hopes of creating from the soil "a new life" for themselves, their families and their countrymen.

175

In the 200 years which have passed since the birth of this nation, it is a sad fact that "this new life" has been unjustly denied the Mexican American. *La vida nueva* is only now becoming a reality for Spanish-speaking citizens of the United States and in our time the dynamic leadership of one man is responsible for restoring their basic human dignity. That man is Cesar Chavez, who worked as a farmworker for most of his life. In recent years, rather than create a poem from the earth as his forefathers had done, Cesar Chavez has labored at planting the seeds of freedom among his fellow Mexican Americans.

In 1927, when Cesar Estrada Chavez was born, his father was trying desperately to scratch out a living for his wife and five children on a small farm near the Colorado River in Yuma, Arizona. After ten years, the soil could no longer support the family so they became migratory agricultural workers trailing the ripening crops from Arizona to California. "Home" was an unending succession of labor camps for the Chavez family. When the camps proved utterly uninhabitable, the back of the family's ramshackle automobile was where they ate and slept. In those days economic depression spread throughout the country and left jobless workers everywhere, but the many Mexican Americans (called *campesinos* and later *chicanos*) with no education, manual skills or land were among the hardest hit. Fatigue, disease and hunger were a familiar part of everyday life for the Chavez family. Every member of the family had to work in the fields just to feed the family the bare minimum, and there was little time for the children's education. Mr. Chavez saw that the vicious cycle of poverty had a firm grip on his family. Their future clearly looked grim and hopeless.

After several personal experiences where the family worked in the fields for days and even weeks without being paid any wages, and after witnessing the similar experiences of other families, he became convinced that the poor workers must band together in some type of structured organization to help one another bargain for fair treatment. Although these first attempts at labor organization met with little success, Mr. Chavez joined every union that came along. He felt sure that labor organization (*la Huelga*) or the strike, if supported, would one day keep his people from being crushed by the injustices they were suffering.

It was during the many days and nights when his father was involved with picketing and strikes, where entire groups of farmworkers would not work at all until pay or working conditions were improved, that Cesar Chavez learned his first lessons about the nature of oppression. He gained keen insight into what could be done about it, along with a clear conviction that it must be alleviated.

When he was 19 years old Cesar Chavez joined the National Agricultural Workers Union, and soon after he left the family to follow the crops on his own. On one of his stops in Delano, California, he met and married his wife, Helen. Not long after, Cesar and Helen Chavez had an unforgettable confrontation with racial prejudice. While sitting in a movie in

Delano, an usherette asked them to leave their seats and move to a section of the theater designated for Mexicans. When they refused to move, the police were called and Cesar Chavez was taken to the police station and arrested for violating the seating policy of the theater: "Mexicans on one side of the aisle . . . and Anglos on the other."

The incident leveled a stunning blow at Cesar Chavez. Although he had for many years suffered the injustice of poor pay for his hard labor, he could see that the discriminatory practices of the theater magnified the unequal status of the Mexican American.

Cesar Chavez continued working the migratory agricultural route throughout the Southwest, but by his mid-twenties he had begun to spend more and more time talking to his fellow workers in an effort to convince them to work cooperatively and constructively to change their economic plight.

Because his formal schooling had never gone beyond the seventh grade, his early attempts to assist his people were often thwarted by his lack of basic education. To remedy the situation, he set out on a course of independent study. He seized every opportunity to improve his reading and writing skills, to learn the history of the labor movement and to perfect the art of organizing workers.

His formal career as a political organizer began while working in the apricot orchards in San Jose, California. There he met a representative of the Community Service Organization (CSO) which at the time was helping disadvantaged Mexican Americans in the area. Although at first very skeptical of the organization because of what the Mexican Americans termed its "gringo" representatives, Cesar Chavez soon recognized the many major contributions the organization had made to his people and became himself an enthusiastic and active member. At first he concentrated on increasing Mexican American voter registration. Then he set up a new service program to deal with the more pressing "bread and butter" problems of the Spanish-speaking community. His program focused on helping unjustly accused Mexicans get out of jail, helping families obtain welfare payments, procuring drivers' licenses for Spanish-speaking people and settling their immigration status with the proper authorities.

After working for the CSO for 10 years and becoming the general director of the entire organization, Cesar Chavez felt that the organization had begun to attract too many middle-class professional people and had become a "prestige organization" rather than one radically committed to mobilizing the poor. He worked within the organization for four more years, however, fervently supporting what he thought was an earnest movement to organize farmers. In 1962, after his farm union proposal was voted down at the CSO convention, Cesar Chavez resigned from the organization.

With the firm belief that poor people are more susceptible to political organization when they see that the organizer is not "better off" than they are, Cesar Chavez and his family took their $2,000 savings and returned to the fields of Delano, California, to start the National Farm Workers Association!

After drawing maps of the small towns and farming camps he methodically proceeded to canvass the valley searching for a nucleus of supporters in each town. Cesar Chavez recalls, "For six months I traveled around, planting an idea. We had a simple questionnaire, a little card with space for name, address and how much the worker thought he should be paid. My wife mimeographed them and we took our kids for two- or three-day jaunts to these towns, distributing the cards door to door."

It was obvious to the poor farmworkers, as they came to know this gentle, soft-spoken man, that he was seeking no personal gain, but was, as no person had ever been, totally dedicated to their welfare. Thousands of responses were sent back to Delano, reflecting their support and trust in his leadership. To devote more time to building his organization, he gave up his work in the fields and the family survived on the few dollars he could earn on weekends digging ditches and the contributions of food from friends.

The membership in the organization had a high turnover that first year, so Chavez centered much attention on refining his methods of communicating with the workers. By distributing leaflets in the fields, by door-to-door contact and more intimate small-group orientation about union goals and objectives, the membership became more cohesive in the second year and initiated an insurance program, a credit union, a special grievance committee to investigate problems of farmworkers and a newspaper, *El Malcriado* (*The Misfit*). Impressed with the idea that a colorful banner might give the movement some impetus, a sense of cultural pride and unique identity, Cesar Chavez studied ancient banners of the past and finally had his cousin make a flag with a black "Aztec eagle" on it to wave at organization gatherings as a symbol of their unity.

From the beginning Cesar Chavez's work as a labor organizer has reflected a deep reverence for human life but it wasn't until he had succeeded in strengthening the bond of solidarity between his people, and they began to demonstrate their unity through *action,* that the effect of his deep religious convictions on the organization he had built became obvious. As a Christian, Cesar Chavez believed that his people would only come to know the peace of real freedom through peaceful means. He was determined that his labor organization be characterized by the total commitment of its membership to nonviolence and negotiation. He seriously studied the writings of Gandhi, the master of nonviolent tactics, and his Christian disciple, Martin Luther King, in an effort to utilize their methods to advance his cause.

He also studied and later made frequent references to the social encyclicals of Pope Leo XIII and Pius IX which defended the inherent dignity of man and the right to strike for better wages and better living conditions. He has also made references on many occasions to the more recent social teachings of Pope John XXIII and Pope Paul VI which have developed the idea of the human dignity of all the minorities throughout the world.

Besides strikes, boycotts, sit-ins and picket lines, Cesar Chavez has encouraged the Catholics in his organization to express their belief in the dignity of man through the traditional religious practices of their faith. Masses, fasts, prayer vigils and processions today continue to provide a natural avenue of expression for their beliefs.

In 1966, Cesar Chavez' original organization, the National Farm Workers Association, merged with another union to form the United Farm Workers Organizing Committee and staged a series of strikes and boycotts, mostly of grapes and lettuce, which has successfully won them the right to act as a collective bargaining agent for thousands of farmworkers.

In 1973 the organization changed its name to the United Farm Workers of America; in November, 1975, they completed 13 months of negotiations with the Coca-Cola Company food division of Florida (Minute Maid Products) over renewal of a contract covering farmworkers at the Minute Maid groves in Lake Alfred, Florida. "Under the contract," U.F.W.A. president, Cesar Chavez, said, "Coca-Cola workers will be the highest paid farmworkers in the southern United States."

Cesar Chavez will continue his work to help *La Vida Nueva* become reality for all Americans.

Recommended Readings

Day, Mark. *Forty Acres: Cesar Chavez and the Farm Worker.* New York: Praeger, 1971.

Dunne, John Gregory. *Delano: The Story of the California Grape Strike.* New York: Farrar, Straus, Giroux, 1967.

Learning Experience
Primary Level

TEACHER NOTES:

When you have related the story of Cesar Chavez' life to the children, bring them to a deeper appreciation of the vital services performed by the United Farm Workers by having ready for examination a large bowl of fresh fruits and vegetables, some canned vegetables and fruits and a jar or two of fruit juice. Ask the children where they think the fruits and vegetables were grown, and who picked them.

LEARNING EXPERIENCE: Handprint

Talk with the children about the good work Cesar Chavez and the farmworkers do with their hands and then have the children make handprints to remind them of that work. Pass out white construction paper to each child and have available a dish with a sponge in it, saturated with tempera paint, so that they can put their hands in the paint and make the imprint of their hands on their construction paper. Help the youngsters to write "helping hands" on their papers and then gather them together for a brief prayer celebration to give praise and thanks for Cesar Chavez and the good work of the many farmworkers in our country. Sing "Thank You, God, For Giving Us Hands." After the children have prayed together for a few moments, share with them the fruits and vegetables you have brought.

SUPPLIES:
Fruits and vegetables, white construction paper, tempera paint, sponge, dish.

Learning Experience
Intermediate Level

Teacher Notes:
After you have related the biography of Cesar Chavez to the youngsters, explore the problems of the migrant farmworker in more depth by showing them one of the following films:

Decision at Delano, 20-min. Roa Films, Inc.
Hunger in America, 52-min. Mass Media Ministries.
Harvest of Shame, 54-min. McGraw-Hill Films.

LEARNING EXPERIENCE: Bulletin Board
Discuss the film at length with the youngsters and then challenge them to share what they have learned by making Cesar Chavez and the farm-workers the subject of a bulletin board in their school or church. Give the youngsters sufficient materials for the project and encourage them to collect magazine and newspaper articles about Cesar Chavez and the farm-workers to add to their bulletin board and to keep it up to date.

SUPPLIES:
Film, construction paper, tape or thumbtacks, scissors, magazine and newspaper articles.

Learning Experience
Junior High Level

TEACHER NOTES:
When the students have had time to explore the biography of Cesar Chavez, talk with them about the problems he, the farmworkers and Spanish-speaking Americans in our country still face daily. Here are a few: housing discrimination, problems due to language and cultural differences, lack of educational and job opportunities, unfair wages.

LEARNING EXPERIENCE: Letters

Discuss with the youngsters the many ways Spanish-speaking Americans are trying through nonviolent means to correct these abuses and then suggest a way they can effectively assist them in their cause. Challenge the students to write letters to their U.S. Senators and Representatives, state and local officials, Church officials and local newspapers urging them to introduce and support legislation and policies which offer equal opportunity for Spanish-speaking Americans and safeguard their civil rights. Remind the students that other minorities (blacks, Orientals, American Indians) suffer many of the same abuses in this country and encourage them to note in their letters the injustices these groups suffer as well.

SUPPLIES:

Paper, pencils, pens.

Paraliturgical Celebration for Unit V
Reshaping the Nation and the World

Theme:

Because Christ really made a difference in the lives of each of the people we have explored in this unit, they were able to respond creatively to the needs of others. In unique ways Alfred E. Smith, Dorothy Day, Thomas Dooley and Cesar Chavez reflect Christlike compassion by using their special talents for public service, healing, and social reform, to eliminate the many different kinds of injustice that exist in the world. Today let us celebrate the spirit with which they shared their gifts in the past and continue to share them today.

Entrance Hymn:

"You Are the Light of the World," Stephen Schwartz, *Godspell,* Celebration Services, Ltd.

Penitential Rite:

For the times I have turned away from you, Lord, and my fellowman to only love and serve myself, Lord, have mercy.

LORD, HAVE MERCY.

For the times I have turned away from a helping hand, a warm smile. . . the glowing light of your love in others, Christ, have mercy.

CHRIST, HAVE MERCY.

For the times I have not shared the joy of your presence with others, Lord, have mercy.

LORD, HAVE MERCY.

First Reading:

(Romans 12:6-9, 12-13)

Gospel Reading:

(Matthew 5:13-17)

Homily:

Comment on how Jesus was present in these Catholic Americans and is present in each of us as we deliver his message of love to others. Help the youngsters to understand that through love and good work others will come to know the hope and utlimate joy of Jesus. Remind them that by letting the light of Jesus' presence shine in them, others will come to know him better.

Song:

"I Believe in You," Joe Wise, *Songs of Praise and Reconciliation,* N.A.L.R.; "We Bring His Holy Love," traditional Negro spiritual; "Yours Is the Kingdom," J. H. Miffleton, *People's Mass Book,* W.L.P.; "It Is Better to Light Just One Little Candle," Shawnee Press.

Meditation:

from *Meditations,* Dorothy Day (Stanley Vishnewski, ed., New York: Newman Press, 1970).
" 'The coat that hangs in your closet belongs to the poor.' And to go further, 'If anyone takes your coat, give him your cloak too.' . . . 'Open your mouth and I will fill it,' says the Lord in the Psalms. The more you give away, the more the Lord will give to you to give." Follow the reading by a recording of "Dear Father" from *Jonathon Livingston Seagull.*

Recessional:

"The Spirit Is A-Movin'," Carey Landry, *Songs of Praise and Reconciliation,* N.A.L.R.; "Priestly People," Lucien Deiss, *People's Mass Book Missal,* W.L.P.; "This Little Light Of Mine," traditional; "Day By Day," Stephen Schwartz, *Godspell,* Celebration Services, Ltd.

A Backward Glance . . . and A Forward Look

The lives of these 21 "great Americans" have given some idea of the roles Catholics played in building our American heritage.

We began with the enthusiastic missionaries who introduced Catholicism to the "New World" in the early 1500's. Because they came from countries where the interests of Church and state were fused, these dedicated and courageous messengers were, for the most part, insensitive to the rich cultures and established traditions of the native Americans. Preaching, educating and baptizing were the natural counterpart of the colonizing efforts of Spain and France and, as a result, the Church achieved enormous success during the next 250 years.

The Spanish missions covered an immense territory—from Florida to northern California—and the missions of New France extended from Quebec and the Great Lakes in the north, through the Mississippi Valley and south to Louisiana. Yet, remarkably, the mainstream of American Catholic life emerged from the minority of Catholics in the English colonies rather than from the state-favored Catholics of the French and Spanish colonies.

Anti-Catholic bias was brought to Jamestown in 1607, and it became visible in the laws and charters of each of the 13 colonies. But, by the time of the Revolutionary War, the loyalty of the Catholics in the colonies, plus the influence of the French alliance, combined to dilute the anti-Catholic prejudice, and the process of eliminating anti-Catholic legislation began. Then, too, there was the prominent Maryland family, the aristocratic Carrolls—two brothers and their cousin—who demonstrated that it was possible to be Roman Catholics and good Americans at the same time!

Daniel Carroll (1730-1796) signed both the Articles of Confederation and the U. S. Constitution; his cousin, Charles Carroll (1737-1832), is remembered as the last surviving signer of the Declaration of Independence. Both held a number of state and national offices during their lifetimes. When Charles Carroll died at the age of 95, he was the richest man in America.

In 1789 American Catholic priests elected the able and talented John Carroll (1735-1815) as the first American bishop of the 25,000 Catholics who were living in this country. They constituted less than one percent of the total population, but a drastic change in that percentile would occur during the next 100 years. Bishop Carroll could not foresee that millions of Catholics would immigrate to this country within the next century and that they would radically alter the nature of American Catholicism.

The children of these immigrants became a powerful political factor especially in large cities such as Boston, Chicago and New York. They began to make their interests known during the presidential election of 1928— their votes supported the democratic nominee who was a Catholic and the governor of New York City, Alfred E. Smith. Though there were other contributing factors, the tradition of anti-Catholic bias played a major part in his defeat. In 1960, when John F. Kennedy decided to run for the presidency, he recalled the fate of Al Smith and openly appealed to the electorate's sense of fair play. He said, "I refuse to believe that I was denied the right to be President on the day I was baptized."

His election and the 1,000 days that followed were a high point for American Catholics. Andrew Greeley says, "On Inauguration Day, 1961, American Catholicism had come full circle. For the first time since the death of Charles Carroll of Carrollton, the most important, the most famous, the most powerful American Catholic was not a member of the hierarchy."* The election of J.F.K. helped us realize that 50 million Americans—now 25 percent of the population—are Catholics, mostly well-educated, successful persons in the mainstream of American culture. Greeley goes on to say, "One hundred forty-five years had passed since the death of John Carroll, and American Catholicism had survived the violent trauma of the immigration experience. It was now once again a legitimately native American Church. . . ."**

Today, we face the challenge of using the best in our religious tradition to build a better America and, in fact, a better world. Are there Catholic Americans consciously, collectively, working on the contribution of the Catholic tradition to the American culture? What is the American Catholics' unique influence on the universal Roman Catholic Church? Where are the Gibbonses, the Englands, the Carrolls, the Cabrinis of tomorrow?

---

* Greeley, Andrew M. *The Catholic Experience,* p. 292.
** *Ibid.,* p. 293.

RECOMMENDED READINGS:

Greeley, Andrew M. *The Catholic Experience*. Garden City, New York: Doubleday, Image Books, 1967.

Fuchs, Lawrence H. *John F. Kennedy and American Catholicism*. Des Moines, Iowa: Meredith Corporation, 1967.

Learning Experience
Primary Level

TEACHER NOTES:

When you have related the information in the conclusion to the children, draw them into a discussion of the Great American Catholics they have studied by first asking which one they most enjoyed learning about and why. In the discussion that follows point out that these Catholics were both men and women, people of many different races and nationalities. Remind them also that, although each of the people chose to serve others in their lifetime, they each chose to do it in a uniquely different way.

LEARNING EXPERIENCE: Portrait Gallery

Pass out white construction paper and invite the children to draw and paint or color a portrait of one or several of the Great American Catholics they have learned about. Mount the "portraits" on colored construction paper and then hang them throughout the classroom, on bulletin boards or in a specific display area. Point out to the children that since each of them is a "Great American Catholic" of the future you would like them each to make a self-portrait and hang it in the classroom as well. Assist the children in making large construction paper letters to spell out "Great American Catholics: Past, Present and Future" and either arrange them on poster paper at the entrance to the classroom or suspend them with string or strong thread from the ceiling in mobile-like fashion.

SUPPLIES:

Construction paper, paint or crayons, scissors, paste or string.

Learning Experience
Intermediate Level

TEACHER NOTES:

Once you have related the information in the conclusion to the youngsters, explain to them that, besides the Catholic Americans whose stories are highlighted here, there are many others who, with Christlike compassion for their fellowman, have made noteworthy contributions in the *past* but *do not* appear in this volume. Also, there are many Catholic Americans *today,* some famous and some not so famous, who either individually or through various organizations witness to the same gospel values.

LEARNING EXPERIENCE:
  Classroom Resource Guide: "More Great American Catholics"

Challenge the children to gather information (from encyclopedias, newspapers, magazines or even personal interviews) about many other Great American Catholics who have in the past or are today witnessing to their faith by showing care and concern for their fellowman. Just a few suggestions of individuals who have made many great contributions but whose lives the youngsters have not explored in this book are: John Ireland, John Hughes, Rose Kennedy, John Nueman, Benedict Flaget, Thomas Merton, Theodore Hesburgh, Andrew Greeley, Geno Baroni. Have the youngsters write brief reports about the people either you or they have selected for them to research. Compile the reports, with illustrations done by the children if possible, in loose-leaf form at a central location in the classroom. Encourage the youngsters to be aware of people in their local community, diocese, or state who are making significant contributions. Invite them to report on them and add the reports to their classroom resource guide from time to time.

SUPPLIES:

Books, magazines, newspapers the youngsters may use to research "More Great American Catholics," paper, loose-leaf notebook.

Learning Experience
Junior High Level

TEACHER NOTES:
    After the students have had time to read and reflect on the conclusion, talk for a few minutes with them about those things that they feel are important for them as American Catholics today. Stimulate the discussion by asking the students to recall the lives of some of the Great American Catholics they have studied. Reflect with them on both the ordinary and the extraordinary things those men and women did in their lives, focusing specifically on what *motivated* their behavior and *why.*

LEARNING EXPERIENCE: Ranking Priorities

Pass to each one of the students the following checklist of items and direct them to "rank" all the items from 1-10. Note that 1 would represent the item they feel is most important in life and 10 the item they feel is of least importance. Reassure the students that they will not be graded on their responses.

Before they begin, tell them to rank all the items in the checklist twice. Their responses under Column A, marked TODAY, should indicate "the way they feel about the items right now," and their responses under Column B, marked MY HOPE FOR TOMORROW, should indicate the way they feel the items would be ranked "if everything were perfect in their lives."

	Column A TODAY	Column B MY HOPE FOR TOMORROW
money		
family		
friends		
country		
job		
education		
member of the opposite sex		
drugs, drinking, smoking		
God		
food		

When the students have finished, either arrange them in small groups with a moderator in each or remain together as a large group and discuss their responses with questions such as the following as a guide: Is there a difference between your responses in Column A and Column B? If so, what is the difference? Why? What are the items that you are happy you valued so highly? Which items would you like to place less value on in your life in the future and why? Can you make any suggestions about how you might place less value on these things at another time in your life? How might changes in your priorities affect your family, friends, wider Community?

Tell the students to leave their checklists unsigned and ask them to pass them in to you. Tally their responses so that they can see how their "priorities" compared with those of their classmates.

Close the class with a brief prayer thanking God for the many gifts he has given us today and asking that we may use them, like the many Great American Catholics we have studied in the past, to make a better tomorrow.

SUPPLIES:
Pencils, pens, "checklist of items."

ADDRESSES FOR SONGS

Celebration Service, Ltd.
Yeldall Manor
Hare Hatch near Twyford
Berkshire RG10 9XR
England

Thomas Y. Crowell Company
666 Fifth Avenue
New York, NY 10019

F.E.L. Publications, Ltd.
1925 Pontius Avenue
Los Angeles, CA 90025

Franciscan Communications Center
1229 S. Santee Street
Los Angeles, CA 90015

G.I.A. Publications, Inc.
7404 S. Mason Avenue
Chicago, IL 60638

North American Liturgy Resources
300 E. McMillan Street
Cincinnati, OH 45219

Oak Publications
33 W. 60th Street
New York, NY 10023

Shawnee Press
Delaware Water Gap, PA 18327

The Word of God Music
P. O. Box 87
Ann Arbor, MI 48107

World Library Publications, Inc.
2145 Central Parkway
Cincinnati, OH 45214

Recommended General Readings

Cogley, John. *Catholic America.* New York: Dial Press, 1973.

Ellis, John Tracy. *American Catholicism.* Chicago: University of Chicago Press, 1969.

Leckie, Robert. *American and Catholic.* Garden City: Doubleday and Company, 1970.

McAvoy, Thomas T., C.S.C. *A History of the Catholic Church in America.* Notre Dame: University of Notre Dame Press, 1969.

McClendon, Jr., James William. *Biography as Theology.* Nashville, Tennessee: Abingdon Press, 1974.

New Catholic Encyclopedia. New York: McGraw-Hill, 1967.